SABOR

Flavours from a Spanish Kitchen

NIEVES BARRAGÁN
MOHACHO

Photography by Chris Terry

PENGUIN
FIG TREE

To my parents

Maria Nieves Mohacho and Pedro Barragán

INTRODUCTION

I come from a family that loves home cooking. Growing up in Santurtzi (Santurce) on the coast near Bilbao, an area famous for its sardines, we would occasionally go out to bars at the weekends, but *pintxos* (what we call tapas in Basque) are expensive and you don't feel as satisfied or full as when you sit down to eat a proper home-cooked meal. Coming home from school or work for lunch, we'd sit down at the table and start to talk about what we were going to have for dinner. When we sat down to dinner, we'd start to talk about what we were going to eat tomorrow for lunch. It was always all about food, food, food.

My mum loved running her house and a big part of that was making sure that her family all ate well. Of course, it's fairly normal for your mum (or maybe your dad) to make lunch and dinner, but for my mother it was about getting the best ingredients and products. They didn't have to be expensive, it was just about selecting them with care. That's what I do in my cooking now: it's all about ingredients and products and finding the very best, whether it's a leek or a tomato. Selecting your ingredients with care is a very Spanish thing. As a child, when I went shopping with my mum on Saturday mornings, she would always say things like, 'Can I have this peach? No, not that one, that one's a little bit bruised, can I have *that* one?' Or, if we were at the fishmonger's, choosing red mullet, she would look at the fishes' eyes and see the one that wasn't so fresh and say, 'No, don't give me that one!' She taught me to be very picky.

When I came home from school, my mum would start to make the dinner and make up a game to keep me entertained. I'd see her preparing things, and she'd say, 'Let's do this,' so I'd pick the parsley, or pod the peas or broad beans – fun jobs that weren't dangerous. Every time my mum tasted what she was cooking, she would give me some too. That's probably why I've never been scared to try anything, because that's what my mum taught me. In our house it was normal to eat livers, brains and sweetbreads.

My family – my mum, dad, brother and grandma – ate proper meals for lunch and dinner. That didn't mean they were really luxurious or cost a lot; my father was a builder and he would come home starving, so my mum always made sure that he was well fed. It wasn't just a case of having one plate of food and that was it. The table would be set with plates, with bowls placed on top. The first thing we ate was always in a bowl, with a spoon – maybe it was soup, or lentils or a stew: something to warm you up. The second course would be fish or meat: something to fill you up. We might have two of my favourites, flat green bean, tomato and potato stew (see page 125), and then braised rabbit (see page 222). Plus salad and maybe a little *jamón*, and always bread. No one would really speak during the first course – except to say, 'Pass me the bread' – because we were all hungry. But by the second course we would start talking and asking about each other's days – and, of course, my mum would ask everyone what they wanted to do for lunch tomorrow . . .

Even when I was in my late teens and going out at the weekends, I was always thinking about eating well. I loved going to a particular restaurant where they served Galician-style octopus on potatoes: it was tapas, and you were eating standing up, but it was a great way to start the evening. I didn't want to eat half a sandwich or a burger – that was for the end of the night. I spent all my money on food and restaurants. I still do.

I never thought I was going to be a chef. My mum used to say that she loved cooking but being a chef was different. Now, of course, it's fashionable: you just have to turn on the TV to see the dozens of cooking shows.

I wasn't sure what I wanted to do: I volunteered in the Red Cross because I liked caring for people, but I loved drawing and cooking too. I hadn't enjoyed training to become a nurse and, when I studied architectural draughtsmanship, I found that every day was the same. So, halfway through my course, I decided to travel for six months, learn a different language and see if I enjoyed working in a kitchen. I came to London, and I fell in love.

One of my friends from home had a boyfriend who worked in a French restaurant called Simply Nico. When I went there to speak with the chef, he said, you don't speak any English, you need to start as a KP. I was ready. I may have been unable to talk, but I showed my enthusiasm and ambition in other ways. If I had to peel the potatoes, I was the fastest at peeling the potatoes. If I had to peel the onions, I was the fastest at peeling the onions. I worked really long hours but everything was new to me and I was happy. After about four weeks, they said, OK, we'll put you on salads. Then I moved to hots . . . and I started to speak English in the kitchen. The only way to really understand how to run a kitchen is to start from the bottom and work your way up, and it was at Nico that I realized that being a head chef isn't just about cooking – in fact, that's almost the easiest part.

Being the only Spanish woman in a French kitchen wasn't always easy. It's a different world now, but at the time I really had to stand my ground. After a period working at Gaudí, a Spanish restaurant (now closed) in Clerkenwell in London – a really happy time in which I made some of my best friends – I moved to Fino, a small restaurant in Fitzrovia that Sam and Eddie Hart opened in 2003. Fino was probably the first proper Spanish restaurant in London and it was there, almost five years after I started working in restaurant kitchens, that I started to cook what I really wanted to: lots of small dishes and little bites packed with flavour, instead of traditional starters and mains. This way of eating has a different vibe: it's less formal, more fun, and there's more opportunity for playing around with ingredients. Working at Fino gave me the confidence to be myself, and I began to cook Spanish recipes with ingredients from the UK at the same time as building relationships with suppliers that enabled me to get amazing Spanish ingredients like goose barnacles (a crustacean that is a delicacy in northern Spain).

Four years after opening Fino, Sam and Eddie opened another restaurant, the first Barrafina on Frith Street in Soho. Again, I planned the menu – it was similar to Fino, but with more of a Basque influence, and more tapas. It was stressful because more dishes equals more ingredients and more to do. On top of this, there were no reservations, meaning we didn't know how many people would show up. I'd always worked in kitchens that were tucked away from sight, and for the first time I was going to have people watching how we were doing everything. The day we opened there was one guy waiting outside, but slowly people started to look through the window and come in. After an hour or so, we were full – although you only needed twenty-three people to fill the restaurant! As soon as I began to cook, I forgot about everyone watching. Over the years the reaction of the customers at Barrafina has taught me so much; I can immediately see when people like something (or don't), and this has helped me to make my recipes better. When the second Barrafina opened on Adelaide Street in Covent Garden in 2014, I wrote a completely new menu.

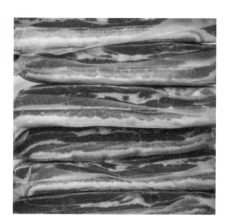

INTRODUCTION

I didn't want to serve the same dishes, because we're not a chain, and that's not my style of cooking. I like when people talk about having a favourite out of the three restaurants (Drury Lane opened in 2015), as they all have their own identity, though they share the same atmosphere and brilliant service. In 2014, Barrafina was awarded a Michelin star. When the founder of Barrafina, Sam Hart, called to tell me, at 7 a.m. or so, I was like, 'What are you talking about?' I didn't think I'd ever have a Michelin star because that's not my style of cooking, and Barrafina isn't a 'Michelin type' of restaurant – although the service is exemplary. It's good that the way people think about these things is changing, though: eating fantastic food doesn't have to be so formal. For me, the point of going out is to have a great time. Barrafina has retained its star for three years now, and the team work so hard and really deserve it.

Sabor means 'flavour' in Spanish, and, above everything, flavour is what defines the food I make. I'm from the Basque country and I love Basque cuisine but I also love travelling around Spain. My food, and by extension the recipes in this book, is inspired by growing up in Santurtzi, but also by my experiences travelling and working in London for more than eighteen years. The combination of ingredients and flavours that I use is the way I try to express these experiences. It's not fusion, but I might mix a traditional Basque recipe with flavours from Galicia and Catalonia – and it works. Conversely, it was moving to another country that made me want to go back to my roots, to really travel around my country and learn more about it, and to be able to transmit its richness and diversity to the people who eat and cook my food. I'll never know, but if I'd stayed in Bilbao I might only be cooking Basque food.

Unsurprisingly, I'm not precious about tradition. The more you travel and the more you taste, the more you discover all the different possibilities there are to cooking. There's never only one way to make something, and no one method is better than another. It might sound obvious, but if I could give one piece of advice about cooking, it would be to be flexible and to cook with what you want to eat. If this means leaving out an ingredient or adding another one, that's fine. People are familiar with classics like tortilla or ham *croquetas*, but I make chorizo tortilla and prawn *croquetas*. For me, it's all about taking one base thing, whether that's béchamel or *alioli*, and expanding it and making it exciting by adding something new.

This might also involve using new ingredients like root vegetables (until recently, you wouldn't see Jerusalem artichokes on Spanish menus, but I love to use them), or it might be about thinking of how to bring Spanish flavours to things that are not traditionally Spanish, like cockles, or skate. My attitude is that as long as what you make is delicious you can have fun finding your own way there. This is at the heart of my food: classic Spanish recipes with fresh flavours.

Most of the recipes in this book are for 4–6 people. That's partly because they work well for these quantities, but it's also because the kind of food I love to cook is sociable. Rather than being individually plated, it works best served on platters, so that everybody can get stuck in and help themselves. For me, it's a happy, interactive way of eating, people saying, 'Pass me this' or 'Pass me that' – you have to get involved. Of course, cooking for 4–6 might not be practical for everyone, and if you want to make a recipe for two you can just halve the quantities in most cases (two exceptions are the *romesco* on page 56 and the *alioli* on page 287, where you need to make enough for the food processor to work).

Cooking is so strange: what I'm cooking today and what I cooked yesterday can turn out so differently. The first thing I ever cooked was a roast chicken (see page 212): it was crisp-skinned and juicy and perfect: my dad couldn't believe it. The next time I made it, a few weeks later, it didn't turn out right. That was a valuable lesson. Cooking isn't a mechanical process: it's about instinct and confidence and learning what something should smell, feel and taste like. Recipe writing is imprecise and difficult to communicate. When you're cooking there can be so many variables. Your ingredients are one: whether it's the size of your red pepper, the thickness of your fillet of fish or the fattiness of your piece of meat. Your tools are another: how hot your oven is (which will affect how long you cook things for), or the size of your pan (which will affect how much oil you need to use, or how long something takes to simmer). Time is another variable: whether you cook your diced onions and vegetables for 10 or 12 minutes is less important than whether you cook them to the stage where they are soft and almost collapsing – this is what will give an extra sweetness and depth of flavour to your stew that will make it really special. Admittedly, desserts are different, as they do generally require precision, and 200ml of double cream is always 200ml of double cream. All I can say is that, as with my roast chicken, the best way to learn is through your mistakes – they are what will teach you to become a better cook.

Spanish cooking – and my cooking – isn't just about learning new techniques but it is all about ingredients and products and making the very best of everything that you use. It's about not covering flavours, but letting them speak for themselves.

MY FAVOURITE INGREDIENTS

GARLIC & PARSLEY

Garlic and parsley are probably the two most important ingredients for me. There was a very famous Basque TV chef, Karlos Arguiñano, who I used to watch every afternoon. He always used to finish the plate of whatever he'd cooked with some parsley leaves: that's a very Basque thing. In the north of Spain, we add garlic and parsley to everything. When you go to the butcher, they chuck a bunch of parsley into your bag for free; my mum would always keep a bunch of parsley in the fridge in a glass of water. Picking parsley leaves and peeling garlic were the first things I learned to do in the kitchen, and 90% of the savoury recipes in this book contain garlic and parsley, whether whole, or in the form of my special oil, *ajillo* (see page 283). Why do I use garlic and parsley so much? Because they enhance the flavour of whatever I'm cooking, without dominating it – unlike smoked paprika (*pimentón*), which is typically associated with Spanish cooking but has a very prominent flavour. You might not be able to discern them but they lift everything they are added to.

WINE & ALCOHOL

When you add alcohol to your cooking, it changes everything. In Spain, we use a lot of alcohol in our cooking, because there's always half a bottle knocking around. A splash of wine or sherry adds an extra element of flavour.

TINNED GOODS

In Spain, our tinned produce – particularly fish – is of very high quality and is priced accordingly. Open any kitchen cupboard and you will be sure to find salted anchovies, *ventresca* (tuna belly), sweet *piquillo* peppers and white asparagus. Make a baguette with *ventresca* and you will be in heaven. Preserving these ingredients is labour-intensive. That's why they are expensive. People have a better understanding of this now, but before they would be like, '£20 for a tin of tuna . . . what?'

Anchovies are hugely important in northern Spain. The season is short (from May to August), so after the fish are caught, time is spent readying them to be preserved. I visited one of the most famous suppliers in the region, Don Bocarte, who produce 4.8 million anchovies a year. Amazingly, their female employees do everything by hand – there are no machines. First, the anchovy heads are removed one by one, then the fish are placed in neat rows in buckets, layered with sea salt. These buckets are kept in a dry store – not a fridge – for a year before they are removed.

SARDIN-ZAHARRA

0,60€/kg

MY FAVOURITE INGREDIENTS

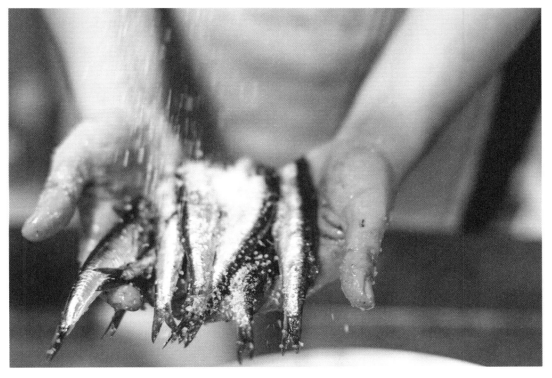

MY FAVOURITE INGREDIENTS

The smell of the cured anchovies is unbelievable. It's nutty, almost like *jamón*. I leant in to smell them, and I didn't want to take my nose away! The salt, which turns a deep brown, is shaken off, and the anchovies are then carefully separated by size before being skinned, deboned and filleted and tinned – careful, painstaking work. At the end of the process, each of the workers places a label that looks like a raffle ticket with her personal number in the tin. That way, if anything is wrong with the anchovies in the tin, the company knows who filled it!

Delis will offer a range of brands, but Ortiz anchovies are also good quality and an affordable price, and are available from many supermarkets now.

When I buy a tin of anchovies, I always keep the oil and use it when making mayonnaise (see page 287) to add extra flavour – you could also use it in salad dressings.

JAMÓN IBÉRICO

Jamón is so important to Spanish food. In a Spanish kitchen, everyone always has some sliced *jamón* in their fridge: it's so easy to put a plate of it on the table, though we also love to use it in baguettes for an amazing sandwich (a *bocadillo*) and, of course, to cook with it.

Jamón ibérico is made from the legs of black Iberian pigs, but the top class is *jamón ibérico de bellota*, which is made from Iberian pigs that have been fed exclusively on acorns for three months in the autumn, during the acorn-foraging season. It has an amazingly sweet and nutty flavour.

There are many different brands of good-quality *jamón ibérico de bellota* available to buy. I like to use 5J (Cinco Jotas), because I have known the producers for many years, and it's well known and is stocked by lots of shops and used by many restaurants. But as long as you buy *jamón ibérico de bellota*, it's going to be good.

We visited a Basque pig producer whose pigs are small, black and white, and weigh maybe 80–90 kilos. These pigs, Euskal Txerria, are a breed facing extinction – in 1980, there were only fifty of them left in the whole country, and nowadays you can find just 130 sows. The pigs we saw are free-range and acorn-fed on a farm near Arruitz, a beautiful place under the care of Bixente Goñi, a farmer with more than forty years of experience.

OLIVE OIL

When you open olive oil, try to use the bottle as soon as possible. It's like perfume: by the time you have a few centimetres left, the flavour is gone.

Arbequina olive oil

Arbequina is a type of very tiny olive from the Catalonia area and Majorca. This is the main olive oil that I use. It is very elegant and clean – some olive oils can be too peppery or bitter, and change the flavour of whatever you add them to. Arbequina complements other ingredients, enhancing their flavour rather than obscuring it. If you can't find it, use a good extra virgin olive oil.

Pomace olive oil

This is a type of oil made from the second pressing of the olive. It allows you to cook at a slightly higher heat without burning or killing the properties of the olive oil. It's widely available, but if you can't find it you can use any light olive oil.

VINEGAR

When I was a child, I used to take the bottle of vinegar and hide from my mum when she was cooking. I'd pour it out into its lid and drink it, I loved it so much. I used to have white lips! My mum never let me dress the salad because I would add too much vinegar. I still love it now, but I don't drink it straight, and though I'm generous with it when I make dressings, I don't add quite as much as I used to.

Moscatel vinegar

My favourite vinegar, Moscatel's sweetness is balanced by its acidity. I almost always use it for dressing salads or raw ingredients.

Jerez vinegar

Stronger and with more of an oaky taste than Moscatel, sherry vinegar is great for cutting through other flavours – I tend to use it when dressing roasted, smoky vegetables.

ARAGÓN OLIVES

I'm not very keen on black olives but I do like Aragón olives, which have a soft and almost creamy texture. I always buy them unpitted.

CHORICEROS (DRIED PEPPERS)

Every kitchen in Spain has a string of dried *choriceros* hanging up. We use them a lot to make sauces like *romesco*, or when marinating or braising. I can't imagine cooking without them – the flavour they give is nutty and rustic and lifts everything else. They keep for a few months. *Ñora* peppers are similar to *choriceros* but smaller and rounder in shape. Their flavour is less smoky, but you can of course use them in place of *choriceros* if you have some.

GUINDILLAS (DRIED PEPPERS)

Guindillas are a type of pepper grown in the Basque country. Long and slim, they add a subtle extra layer of spiciness but are mild enough not to overpower other flavours. Whenever I use dried *choriceros*, I add a *guindilla* too. You can also buy them jarred and pickled: preserved in this way, they make a perfect *pintxo* to have with a drink (see *banderillas*, page 36).

SMOKED PAPRIKA (PIMENTÓN)

It's most common to use smoked sweet paprika, although for a few recipes, like the octopus on page 156, for example, I use smoked hot paprika.

SALT & PEPPER: A NOTE ON SEASONING

It's a simple thing but, whatever you're cooking, seasoning each ingredient slightly as you add it to the pan (rather than seasoning everything at the very end) means it's easier to gauge how much salt you're adding and to ensure that the dish is neither under- nor over-seasoned. It's really difficult to get it right when seasoning large quantities – the key is just to add a little bit as you go.

GENERAL NOTES

- Eggs, unless otherwise specified, are medium.
- Butter, unless otherwise specified, is unsalted.
- I like to finish everything with an extra drizzle of extra virgin olive oil.
- I use sea salt or table salt for adding to boiling water.

MY FAVOURITE INGREDIENTS

STARTERS AND FRIED BITES

In the Basque country, it's common to go to a bar and have a *zurito* (a very small, cold beer) or a glass of wine and maybe a *banderilla* (see page 36), then go on somewhere else. Each bar will do something amazingly well: they might make ten or twenty things, but you go there for one speciality, like the fried stuffed eggs on page 40. By the time you go home you'll often find you're not hungry any more . . . I love going out for *pintxos* (small snacks), but there's no denying that it can be expensive. You might have a plate of artichokes for €7, when you could buy them for less than half that – and they are so easy to prepare (see page 52).

Frying is very common in Spain: it is an essential part of how we cook and eat. People can be apprehensive about frying at home, but the key word here is 'shallow'. You don't need to have a deep fat fryer, or 20 litres of oil, or to mess up your kitchen. My mum never had a fryer and always made *croquetas*, the pig's cheek *empanados* (page 66), *pencas* (page 70) and stuffed eggs (page 40). You can use a regular saucepan if that's what you have, and you don't need more than 2cm of oil – in the restaurant, we call this amount 'two fingers'. Just make sure your oil is hot, add whatever you're frying gently (no splashing!), and turn it round after 2–3 minutes to cook both sides evenly – you don't need to fully submerge it.

I use panko breadcrumbs because I like the texture, but my mum always made her own: she used to keep old bread in a basket and when she had four or five pieces she'd grate it and put it into a container in the dry store. It's easy to do the same if you want: just leave your bread to get as hard as possible, then put it into a food processor if you don't want to grate it. You can use different types of bread, such as rye, for more flavourful crumbs too. One of the reasons I love fried bites so much is that, although they can be a bit fiddly, the actual cooking is done in 5 minutes in just one pan. The hard work has an almost immediate reward – especially when you bite into them. I always season anything fried just before serving, as I like to feel the texture of the sea salt.

The way you eat *pintxos* or tapas is up to you. It's about using your imagination and making the most of what you've got available. At home, I might make the goat's cheese, *sobrasada* and honey on toast (see page 35) for a light lunch or dinner. It's a good standby dish: honey is a cupboard staple, goat's cheese is something you might occasionally have in your fridge, and *sobrasada* has a longer life than fresh meat, meaning you might have some left over. These recipes are all great for a quick bite, or to start a meal, but you could also have two or three dishes for lunch or dinner. They don't have to be painstaking to prepare: nothing could be simpler than a plate of melon and *jamón* (see page 62). A table with a few dishes on it always looks happy and full of colour: you know you're going to eat well and have fun.

PIPARRAS PEPPERS

Piparras are from the Basque region and for me, they are one of the sweetest peppers. Long, thin and elegant in shape, they have the benefit of cooking very quickly. When they are finished with a sprinkling of crunchy sea salt, I could eat them like popcorn. *Gernika* peppers are also a Basque speciality and are slightly larger than *piparras*, with a nutty flavour. Whatever type you use, a bowl of peppers is a perfect way to start a meal, though they are also great served alongside a piece of meat or fish – you really don't need anything else.

extra virgin
olive oil

500g *piparras*
(see page 292)

sea salt

Pour ½cm of olive oil into a frying pan and put on a medium heat. When hot, add the *piparras*, turning them with metal tongs – as soon as they start to get some colour (30–40 seconds), they're done. Remove and drain on kitchen paper, then serve, with sea salt sprinkled over.

STUFFED *PIQUILLO* PEPPERS WITH *BUTIFARRA,* PRAWNS & MUSHROOMS

FOR 4

These peppers are an explosion of flavour! *Butifarra* is a white pork meat sausage from Catalonia. There are two types: fresh, like a normal sausage, and already boiled, which you can just slice. This recipe uses the second kind, though the fresh *butifarra* would be nice as well.

200g wild mushrooms (chanterelles, trompettes, pied de mouton/hedgehog, portobello)

25g *butifarra*

8 medium shell-on raw prawns, peeled and deveined

2 shallots, chopped

8 whole *piquillo* peppers, from a tin

extra virgin olive oil

2 cloves of garlic, chopped

3 tablespoons finely chopped fresh chives

2 tablespoons finely chopped fresh parsley

sea salt and freshly ground black pepper

2 eggs, whisked

100g plain flour

For the salad

½ a bunch of fresh flat-leaf parsley

½ a bunch of watercress

1 red onion, very finely sliced

20ml extra virgin olive oil

10ml Moscatel vinegar

Clean the mushrooms to get rid of any dirt or grit: some people use a brush, but I think the best way is to dab them carefully with a J-cloth.

Chop the *butifarra*, prawns, shallots and mushrooms into 2cm x 2cm cubes. Drain the *piquillos* and scoop out their seeds.

Pour 1 tablespoon of olive oil into a pan over a medium heat and, when hot, fry the mushrooms until the water disappears. Cook for another 30 seconds to caramelize slightly, then add the garlic and cook for 30 seconds before adding the shallots and cooking gently for 1½ minutes. Add the *butifarra* and fry for around 1½ minutes more – you don't want it to get dry. Turn the heat down to medium-low, then add the prawns. Add the herbs, season with salt and pepper and stir everything together, then turn the heat off. Leave to cool.

Stuff the mixture into the *piquillos* using a tablespoon (or a piping bag if you have one). Don't fill them completely – you need to leave some space at the top to squeeze them closed.

Prepare the salad: pick the parsley leaves and mix them with the watercress and red onion. Whisk the oil, vinegar and some salt and pepper together to make the dressing, but hold off combining it with the leaves until the last minute.

Dip the *piquillos* in egg and then in flour to coat. Heat 1–2cm of olive oil in a pan and fry the *piquillos* for a couple of minutes on each side. Remove from the pan and drain on kitchen paper.

Season the peppers and serve with the dressed salad.

GOAT'S CHEESE, SOBRASADA
& HONEY ON TOAST

Sobrasada is a soft cured sausage that comes in a ball – like a spreadable chorizo, or the Italian 'nduja. The combination of the spicy, fatty sausage, salty cheese and sweet honey makes this almost like a savoury dessert. You can use any type of bread for this recipe, but something not too heavy will work best.

Sometimes we make *sobrasada croquetas* at Barrafina: just add 2 or 3 tablespoons of *sobrasada* to a white béchamel. The *sobrasada* will melt into it and in 10 minutes you will have a spicy béchamel to make the most amazing *croquetas* with.

150g
sobrasada

1 slice of *pan de cristal*, *pan de coca*, or other thinly sliced bread per person

1 tablespoon extra virgin olive oil

2 shallots, very finely chopped

1 pinch of fresh thyme leaves

100ml sherry

500g goat's cheese

100ml orange blossom honey

sea salt and white pepper

Remove the *sobrasada* from the fridge and leave it to come to room temperature so that it's easier to spread.

Preheat the oven to 180°C.

Toast the bread in a toaster or under the grill until golden brown on both sides.

Heat the olive oil in a pan on a medium-low heat and cook the shallot gently with the thyme until it's very soft and sweet, but without any colour. Add the sherry and cook until the alcohol has evaporated. Put the contents of the pan into a food processor with the goat's cheese and blend to make a creamy paste.

Add the mousse-y goat's cheese to the toast, then spread the *sobrasada* on top. Bake for 1–1½ minutes maximum – you want the toasts to be warm but you don't want the cheese to split or the *sobrasada* to become too oily.

Remove from the oven and drizzle with the orange blossom honey, then season with white pepper and a little bit of sea salt – it's nice to feel that crunch.

BANDERILLAS

A *banderilla* is a skewer of olives, green chillies and anchovy. You can add pretty much anything to these three base ingredients – there are millions of different types.

In Bilbao, there are bars where the only food they serve is *banderillas*. They go perfectly with your first *zurito* (a very cold, small beer that you drink in two sips, typical of northern Spain), as they are easy to eat, salty and pickle-y. Plus, they make you more thirsty . . .

Peperoncini peppers are spicy, sour and sweet: you should be able to find them in Spanish and Italian delis, but if you can't, then jarred pickled red peppers or chillies are a fine substitute. What you're looking for is that balance between spice and sourness.

24 pitted manzanilla olives

12 pickled *guindilla* chillies

3 spicy red *peperoncini* peppers, quartered

12 salted anchovies

a drizzle of extra virgin olive oil

toothpicks, to serve

Optional

12 soft-boiled quail eggs

100g cured tinned tuna in oil

12 cooked prawns, peeled and deveined

Thread the ingredients on to toothpicks: first an olive, then a pickled chilli, another olive and the spicy red pepper. The last thing is always the anchovy/quail egg/tuna/prawn (so that it's the first thing you put in your mouth). Drizzle with a little olive oil.

A *banderilla* is meant to be eaten in one mouthful so you get everything together.

MEDJOOL DATE, ALMOND &
SMOKED PANCETTA BONBONS

FOR 6 (MAKES 12)

This is another one-mouthful bite: it's sweet from the date and salty from the almonds, with the smoked pancetta adding a crispy texture. Pre-pitted dates can be dry, so try to buy ones with the stones still in. It's important that the pancetta is very thinly sliced, otherwise it will unfurl when you fry it.

12 whole
Medjool dates

24 Marcona
almonds

24 rashers
of smoked
pancetta, very
thinly sliced

rapeseed or
sunflower oil, for
shallow-frying

toothpicks,
to serve

Pit your dates, then put a couple of almonds into the centre of each one and close them. Wrap a couple of slices of pancetta around each date and secure with a toothpick.

Heat some oil in a pan and shallow-fry the wrapped dates until the pancetta is golden and crispy. Remove from the pan and drain on kitchen paper before serving.

STARTERS & FRIED BITES

STUFFED EGGS

Whenever I go out on the weekend with my parents in Santurtzi, we see this old lady who has been making these stuffed eggs at a bar called Lagun Etxea for years. She's famous for it and makes thousands a day. People queue to eat her fried stuffed eggs. They fight for them; it's insane. When you bite into them, all the béchamel starts to come out into the bread. It's messy, but it's a great snack.

I always boil eggs in boiling water: if you start from cold, the yolk will not sit in the centre of the egg and when you come to slice it in half, one side of the white will be much thinner, which is no good for stuffing.

You need to make a minimum of 1 litre of béchamel at a time, so you might have some left over, but you can freeze it, or use it as an excuse to make *croquetas*.

For the béchamel

1 litre whole milk

120g unsalted butter

110g plain flour

sea salt and freshly ground black pepper

a pinch of grated nutmeg

200g honey ham, chopped

For the eggs

8 medium eggs

150g plain flour, to dust

rapeseed or sunflower oil, for shallow-frying

12 slices of baguette, 1½cm thick

sea salt and freshly ground black pepper

a pinch of smoked paprika

To make the béchamel, warm the milk in a pan over a low heat. Put the butter into a separate pan and let it melt on a low heat. When the butter is melted (don't let it colour), add the flour and mix together well, then cook for 1 minute. Add the warmed milk: start with a quarter of it at first, stirring continuously, then add another quarter and keep stirring. Continue cooking and stirring until you've used up all the milk. Adding it little by little keeps the béchamel thick and creamy. You need to cook béchamel for 20 minutes to cook off the flour. Season, mix in the grated nutmeg and chopped honey ham, then remove from the heat.

Whisk 2 of the eggs in a bowl and set aside. Boil the rest of the eggs for 7 minutes in boiling water. Peel under cold running water, then cut them in half. Carefully remove the yolks, then chop them and add to the béchamel, mixing together to incorporate. Once the béchamel mixture is cool, spoon it into the egg halves to fill them. Cover the filled eggs and leave in the fridge until set. When the eggs are set, remove and dip completely first into the whisked egg, then into the flour. Heat the oil in a high-sided pan on a medium heat and shallow-fry the eggs until golden and crispy.

Place the eggs on slices of bread to make *pintxos*. Dust with salt and pepper and a little smoked paprika.

IDIAZABAL CHEESE, WALNUTS & HONEY

Everyone is familiar with Manchego now, but the Basque cheese Idiazabal is less well known – though you can find it in good cheesemongers, delis and food markets. Like Manchego, it is unpasteurized and made from sheep's milk and traditional (animal) rennet. Unlike Manchego, the rind is edible. The most famous type of Idiazabal is smoked and pale yellow in colour, but it is also available unsmoked, and this is the version I prefer. It has a creamy, elegant taste and a different texture depending on how long it is aged: you can choose between 18 months, 12 months and 8 months. I've seen how it's made, and the process really couldn't be more simple. Legend has it that the method was discovered by chance hundreds of years ago, when milk was transported in animal-skin bags, causing the formation of curds. The technique of smoking was also a happy accident apparently, the result of a stored Idiazabal being caught in a house fire that was, luckily, extinguished. For whatever reason, after the cheese was rescued from its shelf someone opened it and tasted it, and discovered that it was delicious!

The classic Basque way to eat Idiazabal is with walnuts and honey – like the *cuajada* on page 262. You can eat it as a light starter or snack, or as a cheese course after dinner. Sometimes, if my father is tired, or eating late, he will sit down at the table and use a small knife to cut pieces of cheese on to his plate, then he'll crack a walnut and that's his dinner. You can also pop a slice of the cheese into your *bocadillo* (sandwich).

STARTERS & FRIED BITES

PRAWNS COOKED IN SALT

This is a simple but nice way to cook prawns, very common in Spain; it doesn't use any oil and ensures the prawns don't lose any of their juiciness. It respects the prawn. The end result is not too salty, as the prawns only take in what they need. If you keep some prawns in your freezer, this is a great speedy dish to have up your sleeve.

1kg good-quality shell-on raw prawns (20–30)

rock salt, enough to make a ½cm thick bed

Put a thin layer of rock salt into a frying pan or on a griddle, as if you are making a salty bed, then lay the prawns on top.

Put on a medium heat and cook for 1 minute for small prawns or 2–3 minutes for larger prawns. Look at the side of the prawn as it cooks: when the line showing that the colour has changed is halfway up the prawn, it's time to turn them.

Shake them off in the pan to remove any excess salt, and pile on to a plate.

CRAB BUNS

Small buttery brioche buns are ideal for this – you don't want big, floury burger buns.

You can cook the crab and pick the meat yourself, then use the shells to make a stock, or buy ready-picked crabmeat and make a stock from small crabs or prawn shells – I have included instructions for both options. Picking the crab is the most time-consuming part of this recipe, so buying it ready-picked is a good option. However, even if you have bought your crabmeat already picked, it's really important to feel through it with your fingers for any little bits of shell, as it's never guaranteed that it will be completely shell-free.

You can make the white bisque in advance and refrigerate it, but you will need to eat it within 2–3 days.

1 x 500g crab, or around 150g ready-picked crabmeat

sea salt and freshly ground black pepper

200g cavolo nero

6 small buttery buns

For the white bisque

a drizzle of extra virgin olive oil (around 1½ tablespoons)

1 clove of garlic, sliced very thinly

2 shallots, finely diced

1 bay leaf

100ml brandy

100ml sherry or white wine

500ml crab stock or prawn stock (see page 288)

250ml double cream

sea salt and freshly ground black pepper, to taste

If you are cooking your crab, put it into a pan filled with cold salted water (you start cooking it from cold so that the crab cooks more gently) and bring to the boil. I normally work to 12 minutes per pound (450g) of crab weight. So, if your crab is around 500g, it will need boiling for about 14–15 minutes. Remove it from the water and leave to cool before picking the meat.

To make the white bisque, pour a drizzle of olive oil into another pan and put on a low-medium heat. Add the garlic and shallots and let them cook down – you want them to be soft, but not browned. Add the bay leaf, brandy and sherry. Cook to evaporate the alcohol, then add the stock. Reduce by about five or six times: you want it to get really thick so there will be very little left in the pan – it will be almost like a glaze. At this point, add the double cream and reduce by half. Season to taste. Turn off the heat and leave the bisque to infuse for 15–20 minutes (this will make it more flavourful), then pass it through a sieve. When the bisque cools down it will be very compact – you should be able to scoop it like ice cream.

To prepare the cavolo nero, cut out the thick, woody stalk at the bottom third of the leaf. Blanch the leaves in boiling salted water for around 2–3 minutes, so that they are very soft, almost overcooked. Remove them to a bowl of iced water to prevent them from continuing to cook and to keep them green. Rinse and dry the leaves, then cut them widthways into 3cm strips.

Add the crabmeat to the white bisque and season to taste. At the last minute add the cavolo nero and mix to combine.

Split and toast the buns, then spoon in the crab/cavolo nero mixture and serve.

SALTED ANCHOVIES & LARDO ON TOAST
FOR 4

When I'm making toast, I like to use a very thin bread called *pan de cristal* or *pan de coca* that you can buy from Brindisa and other Spanish shops. It's not like biting into regular toast, it's very airy and crisp and doesn't fill you up too much – it's similar to ciabatta, but not as thick. When you are eating *pintxos*, you don't want the main taste to be the bread, but what's on top of it – in this case, the anchovies and lardo. The bread is there to add texture and to catch any juices.

If you do buy *pan de cristal* or *pan de coca*, you can freeze it, although you can also use ciabatta, or other good bread, if you like.

2 thin (1cm) slices of *pan de cristal*, *pan de coca* or other bread, toasted

8–12 paper-thin slices of lardo (you can marinate it yourself, with salt, fennel seeds and black pepper, or you can find lots of different types available from butchers or markets)

16 salted anchovies

a bunch (around 200g) of watercress or land cress

60ml extra virgin olive oil, plus extra to serve

25ml Moscatel vinegar

sea salt and freshly ground black pepper

Cut the bread in half lengthways and lightly toast it. Each slice should be around 10–12cm – in the kitchen we call this size 'four fingers'.

Put the lardo on the toast (there should be enough lardo to cover each slice and for you to really feel you are eating lardo!), then cover each with 4 anchovies.

Dress the peppery leaves with the olive oil, vinegar, salt and pepper. Put the leaves on a plate, then place the toasts on top and dress with more olive oil and salt.

SARDINES, GAZPACHO & RED ONION SALAD ON TOAST
FOR 4 (2 SARDINES EACH)

Until as recently as the late 1980s, women in Santurtzi – *sardineras* – used to sell live sardines from big baskets that they carried on their heads. There's even a statue of a *sardinera*, the Monumento a la Sardinera.

Santurtzi is 15 kilometres away from Bilbao, on the coast, and every summer there's a festival where all the restaurants cook sardines over charcoal in the streets. You can smell the smoke for miles; the entire town smells of sardines!

Sardines are a really oily, juicy fish, especially in summer, when they're in season. Traditionally, you place the grilled sardines on a piece of bread, then turn them so their juices soak into the bread. You eat one side of the fish, then turn it and eat the other, chuck the bones and eat the bread. It's the simplest thing but so good – I could have twenty of them. This is my version of the classic.

8 sardines (scales on and guts in)

sea salt and freshly ground black pepper

½ a red onion, cut into thin julienne

½ a bunch of fresh flat-leaf parsley, leaves picked and chopped

20ml extra virgin olive oil, plus an extra drizzle for the bread

10ml Moscatel vinegar

4 slices of good bread

ajillo (see page 283), 1 spoonful per sardine

For the gazpacho

3 bunches of spring onions, white parts only, roughly sliced

1 red pepper, roughly diced

2 cloves of garlic, sliced

½ a cucumber, peeled and deseeded, roughly diced

8 ripe regular size tomatoes, roughly diced

½ a loaf of bread, dough only, ripped up

300ml extra virgin olive oil

sea salt and freshly ground black pepper

75ml sherry vinegar

To make the gazpacho, put all the ingredients into a bowl, mix together and leave overnight. The next day, place everything in a blender and blend until very smooth, then pass through a sieve.

Season the sardines with salt and pepper. Cook them on a griddle pan or barbecue them over charcoal.

Mix together the red onion, parsley, olive oil and vinegar, and season with salt and pepper.

Heat a little oil in a griddle pan on a medium heat and toast both sides of the bread until nice and golden brown – you get more contact this way than using a toaster.

Spoon a little of the gazpacho on to the toast, then top with the onion and parsley salad and the grilled sardines and *ajillo*.

STARTERS & FRIED BITES

EL MANDANGA, HOGAR DEL PESCADOR, SANTURTZI

PAN-FRIED ARTICHOKES & JAMÓN

Pan-frying is a nice, quick way to eat baby artichokes – when they are super-fresh it is best to eat them slightly al dente anyway. If you can't find baby artichokes, you can also make this with green or flat beans.

It's important to have all your ingredients ready before you get going: this recipe takes less than 5 minutes to cook, so you need everything to hand. Cleaning artichokes is one of my favourite kitchen tasks – I find it really therapeutic.

4 shallots, finely diced

2 cloves of garlic, sliced very thinly

4 tablespoons finely chopped fresh flat-leaf parsley leaves

4 slices of *jamón* (Serrano is perfect for this, as it is not too expensive), cut into thick finger-sized strips

40ml extra virgin olive oil, plus another 2 teaspoons to finish

1 teaspoon fresh lemon thyme leaves

sea salt and freshly ground black pepper

juice of ½ a lemon, to finish

For the artichokes

8 very fresh baby artichokes

juice of 2½ lemons

a handful of fresh flat-leaf parsley stalks

To prepare the artichokes, first remove the top two layers of the leaves, then cut off the top third of the artichoke. With a small knife or a peeler, peel the artichokes from the bottom of the stalk to the top: you don't want to be able to see any dark green, just the pale layer underneath.

Put the peeled artichokes into a large bowl of water with the juice of the 2½ lemons and the parsley stalks: these will stop the artichokes discolouring while you prepare the rest. Leave for 20–30 minutes. (Meanwhile, you can prepare the shallots, garlic, parsley leaves and *jamón*.)

Rinse the artichokes thoroughly. If they are small, cut them in half lengthways; if they are larger, cut them in quarters lengthways. Looking at the size of the stalk is a good guide for judging this: you don't want to cut it so thin that when you fry the artichokes the stalks disappear.

Heat the olive oil in a large pan on a medium heat and, when it starts to get hot, add the artichokes. Keep them moving constantly and, when they start to turn slightly golden brown, add the garlic. Sweat slightly, then add the shallots and fry for 30 seconds or so. Now add the *jamón* – turn it with a spoon about four times, then switch off the heat. Add the parsley leaves and lemon thyme, drizzle with more olive oil, season with salt and pepper, then squeeze over the lemon and toss together.

CALÇOTS IN TEMPURA

It's nice to do something different with calçots sometimes, and this tempura method works really well. I normally don't measure the ingredients for tempura batter: you need equal quantities of plain flour and cornflour and enough water to make it smooth. Dip your finger in the mixture: when the batter drops off, it's good. Anybody can make these at home: you don't need a deep fryer.

4 calçots (see page 56) (or use good-quality spring onions, baby leeks or asparagus, when calçots aren't in season)

rapeseed or sunflower oil, for shallow-frying

For the tempura batter

100g plain flour

100g cornflour

400ml very cold sparkling water

sea salt and freshly ground black pepper

To serve

smoked chilli *alioli* (add 3 tablespoons Mexican smoked chilli paste to the *alioli* recipe on page 287)

Remove the first couple of layers of the calçots and clean them thoroughly, the way you would leeks, to get rid of any dirt.

Bring a large pan of slightly salted water to the boil and blanch the calçots until soft, then remove them to a large bowl of iced water.

Make the tempura batter by whisking all the ingredients together, then cover and chill in the fridge until cold (the colder the tempura batter, the more crunchy cracks it will make when it comes into contact with the hot oil).

Cut each calçot into three, so they fit in your pan. Pour a couple of centimetres of rapeseed oil into a high-sided pan or sauté pan on a medium heat and leave to get hot.

Dip the calçots into the batter, then slowly lower them into the pan, stroking the bottom forward into the oil a few times before laying the calçot down, away from you. Doing this means the bottom of the calçot builds up a crust so it won't stick to the pan and also ensures that the oil doesn't splash towards you. Repeat, ensuring that the calçots have enough space to become crispy and golden brown (you will probably need to do three or so batches, depending on the size of your pan). Cook for around a minute and a half, then remove with a slotted spoon and drain on kitchen paper.

Season with salt and pepper and serve with the smoked chilli *alioli*.

A FEAST OF CALÇOTS with ROMESCO

Calçots are in between a fat spring onion and a baby leek. In Catalonia, the best calçots start around December and go on for 2 or 3 months. There is a festival (*calcotada*) in January and a competition in Barcelona to see who can eat the most calçots: someone recently ate close to 300!

The traditional way to cook calçots is to burn them over charcoal until they are completely black. Then you wrap them in newspaper and seal them in a box – this loosens the charred outside and cooks the inside a bit more. To eat them, unwrap them, squeeze the bottom of each calçot with one hand, pull the inside out from the top with your other hand, then drop it into your mouth. It's messy – when you go to eat calçots in a restaurant, they make you wear a bib. The flavour is smoky and juicy . . . so much better than blanching and grilling. It's the best thing. Having a calçot festival at home is such a fun thing to do – you can cook and eat as many as you like.

There are lots of different types of *romesco* sauce: some people use hazelnuts too, but I normally just use almonds. You need to make around 500g or it just doesn't blend together properly. Any extra *romesco* can be kept covered in the fridge for up to 4 days – it goes with pretty much anything, so it won't last long.

calçots – allow around 8–10 per person

For the *romesco* (makes around 500g)

3 whole heads of garlic

250ml extra virgin olive oil, plus more for the garlic, tomatoes and bread

sea salt and freshly ground black pepper

200g whole blanched almonds

6–8 fresh ripe plum tomatoes

2 slices of stale bread

1–2 dried chillies (depending on their size), soaked in warm water for a couple of hours

3–4 dried *choricero* peppers (depending on their size), soaked in warm water for a couple of hours

100ml sherry vinegar

First, you need to roast all the ingredients for the *romesco*. Preheat the oven to 170–180°C. Cut the garlic in half crossways and place it on a large piece of foil. Sprinkle with olive oil, salt and pepper and fold over the foil to close. Roast for 20 minutes, until very soft, then squeeze out all the cloves.

Put the almonds on a baking tray in a single layer and roast in the oven until light golden brown (around 6–7 minutes).

Remove the core from the tomatoes with a small knife, place on a roasting tray with a good drizzle of olive oil, salt and pepper, and roast for 8–10 minutes. The tomatoes will start to break down and lose their liquid and the juices will colour with the olive oil.

Put 1cm of oil into a pan on a medium heat and fry the bread until golden brown on both sides – it should be toasted and have absorbed all the oil.

Put the tomatoes (with their skins) into a blender with the garlic, chillies and *choriceros*, the 250ml of olive oil and the vinegar, and blend to make a dark, thick paste. Rip up the toasted bread and add along with salt, pepper and the almonds. Pulse to blend, so that it comes together but you keep some texture – if you want it to be creamier, keep blending. Keep it warm until you need it.

To cook the calçots, fire up your barbecue. As soon as you have flames, add the calçots and cook until the outside layer is blackened and burnt. Remove from the barbecue, wrap in newspaper and leave them to sit for 20 minutes – they will continue to steam, cooking inside the paper.

Unwrap, take a calçot and hold it by the green end, then pull the top two burnt layers down over its head and discard: you will be left with the soft, sweet interior. Dip this into the romesco, then dangle it down into your mouth and eat. Repeat!

CRISPY PRAWN, *PIQUILLO* PEPPER & PANCETTA ROLL

If you go to San Sebastián or the Basque country you will often find this served as a *pintxo*; it's the perfect starter or snack with a glass of wine.

12 regular-sized prawns, peeled and deveined, tail kept on

12–18 *piquillo* peppers from a jar, opened out and seeds removed

24 slices of smoked pancetta (ask your butcher to cut it very thinly)

100g plain flour

2 eggs, whisked

100g panko breadcrumbs

rapeseed or sunflower oil, for shallow-frying

sea salt and freshly ground black pepper

Take a prawn and wrap a *piquillo* round it (you might need to use 1½ *piquillos* to make sure you are completely covering the prawn), then wrap the pancetta around the *piquillo* so you cannot see any pepper – the fat of the pancetta should hold it together as it overlaps. Dip it in flour, to cover, then in egg and panko. Repeat with the remaining prawns.

Pour some oil into a high-sided pan or sauté pan and put on a medium-low heat. When the oil is hot, shallow-fry the rolls – they will be quite thick, so the heat needs to be gentle enough that the prawn in the centre cooks through without the breadcrumbs colouring too much. Drain on kitchen paper, season with salt and pepper, and serve.

CHISTORRA WITH **CIDER**

Chistorra is a type of chorizo typical to the Basque country and north-east Spain; it is slimmer than regular chorizo and does not contain as much paprika. You can buy it fresh or cured, and you can find it in Spanish shops or online from specialist retailers like Brindisa. Cooked with cider, it makes a punchy sweet and spicy stew.

It's very difficult to get this wrong if you have good sausages and cider – it's so simple and it's the perfect way to start a meal, along with *banderillas* (see page 36).

Mini *chistorra* are perfect for this – and you can get them in lots of places now – otherwise you should slice the sausage into 3cm x 2cm bite-size pieces.

20ml extra virgin olive oil

400g *chistorra* or chorizo

560ml Asturian cider (or other good-quality cider)

sea salt and freshly ground black pepper

toothpicks, to serve

sliced bread, toasted, to serve

Put the olive oil into a pan on a medium heat and add the *chistorra*. Cook for 2–3 minutes, stirring. When it starts to get golden brown and give up its fat, add the cider and reduce by half, until you see that the liquid has emulsified to make a sauce. Taste the sauce and season with salt and pepper if necessary.

Serve warm in little bowls, with toothpicks and pieces of toast.

STUFFED MUSSELS

This is a traditional *pintxo*. Its Spanish name, *tigres*, meaning 'tigers', comes from the yellow and black stripes of the mussels after frying. There are a few steps involved but they aren't complicated.

1kg mussels

1 bay leaf

800ml whole milk

50ml extra virgin olive oil

2 large onions, very finely chopped

sea salt and freshly ground black pepper

150ml white wine

240g unsalted butter

420g plain flour

1 bunch of fresh chives, chopped

1 teaspoon cayenne pepper

1 tablespoon chopped garlic

1 tablespoon chopped fresh flat-leaf parsley

300g panko breadcrumbs

4 eggs, whisked

rapeseed or sunflower oil, for shallow-frying

Pour a little water into a shallow casserole pan and put on a medium heat. When hot, add the mussels and bay leaf, cover with a lid and steam until they open. Put a sieve over a large bowl and drain, collecting the mussel cooking juice. When cool, mix this into the milk and set it aside for the béchamel.

Pick the mussels from their shells. Keep the best-looking halves of the shells.

Put the olive oil into a pan on a medium heat. When hot, add the onions and gently cook them until very soft and sweet but not coloured.

Chop the mussels, then add to the onions, season and stir together. Add the wine and cook to evaporate. Add the butter and melt, then add 220g of the flour and mix together. Slowly add the mussel juice and milk little by little, stirring continuously until you have a béchamel consistency. Add the chives, season and mix to combine. Leave to cool down.

Spoon the béchamel-mussel mix into the reserved mussel shells, giving them a slightly rounded shape. The mixture should be cool enough to be set, but if it's very warm you might need to chill them in the fridge.

Mix the cayenne pepper, garlic and parsley through the panko.

Dip the tops of the mussels in the remaining 200g of flour, the egg and the panko (don't dip the bottom).

Pour some rapeseed or sunflower oil into a high-sided pan or sauté pan and place on a medium-low heat. When hot, shallow-fry the mussels until golden. Remove from the pan with a spoon and drain on kitchen paper. Season and serve.

MELON & JAMÓN

This is all about the balance of the salty ham and sweet melon, so try to find a good melon – *piel de sapo* (meaning 'toad skin', named for its thick, uneven green skin) is the classic Spanish melon – or allow time for it to ripen at home.

It may not seem like a recipe, but this is the perfect thing to put in the middle of the table to start a meal, and anyone can make it.

1 ripe green Spanish *piel de sapo* melon, or other sweet, ripe melon

240g *jamón ibérico de bellota* (I like to use 5J – see page 22), sliced very thinly

40ml extra virgin olive oil

freshly ground black pepper (you shouldn't need any salt, as the *jamón* is salty enough)

Cut the melon into wedges and remove the skin. Cut into large cubes, bearing in mind that each cube should be able to fit into your mouth.

Place the cubes of melon on the serving plate with the ham on top, and finish with the olive oil and pepper.

RUSSIAN SALAD

Ensaladilla rusa is a great starter and the star of the show whenever we make it at home. I've never met a Spanish person who doesn't love it; in fact, everyone loves this salad. It tastes ten times better the next day, chilled, making it good for preparing ahead. I could eat it straight from the fridge.

Try to get small potatoes that are as similar in size as possible: you want them to cook quickly without becoming floury. Cooking them in their skins also stops them turning mushy.

It's important that the potatoes and carrots are still warm when you mix them with the other ingredients, as this helps them to better absorb the flavour of everything.

This is a recipe that makes the most of store-cupboard ingredients: white asparagus and *piquillo* peppers should be from a jar, as should, dare I say it, the mayonnaise.

500g baby potatoes, unpeeled

2 medium-sized carrots, unpeeled

2 eggs

1 Little Gem lettuce, julienned

250g good-quality tinned tuna or bonito in olive oil

300ml mayonnaise, homemade or shop-bought

sea salt and freshly ground black pepper

3 tablespoons chopped fresh flat-leaf parsley leaves

To finish

4 tinned white asparagus spears, cut in half

3 *piquillo* peppers, cut into strips

12 green olives, sliced in half

Put the potatoes into a large pan of cold salted water. Put the pan on a medium heat and bring to the boil – when bubbling, add the carrots and eggs. Remove the eggs after 10 minutes. How long you cook the carrots and potatoes will depend on what size they are – it may be that the potatoes are ready first if they are very small. What you are looking for is for them both to be nice and soft – pierce with a toothpick if you want to check.

Using a slotted spoon, remove the vegetables to a colander to drain. Leave them to cool enough to handle, then peel off the skin with a small knife when they are still warm.

Cut everything into 2cm cubes – potatoes, carrots, eggs – and put them into a large bowl with the Little Gem. Spoon the tuna and its oil into the bowl. Add the mayonnaise, salt and pepper and parsley and mix together.

Spoon on to your serving dish – you want it to be almost cake-like. Then dress the salad with the white asparagus, *piquillo* peppers and olives.

PIG'S CHEEK *EMPANADOS*

FOR 4–6 (A COUPLE OF CHEEKS PER PERSON)

Iberian pig's cheeks are ideal for this recipe, though you could also use ox cheeks (cut into pieces, as they are larger), or veal cheeks. Whatever you use, these *empanados* should be crispy on the outside ('*empanados*' refers to the breadcrumbed exterior) and juicy within. Served with the gravy-like sauce for dipping, they are a really good bite and an amazing start to any meal. If the frying seems like a bit too much effort, or you want to make this the main event, you can easily serve the braised cheeks as a stand-alone stew (this goes really well with the cauliflower with salted almonds, shallot and chilli on page 126).

To braise the cheeks

a drizzle of extra virgin olive oil

12 pig's cheeks

sea salt and freshly ground black pepper

4 carrots, finely chopped

4 sticks of celery, finely chopped

2 leeks, finely chopped

1 onion, finely chopped

2 bay leaves

½ a bunch of fresh thyme

½ a bottle of red wine

1½ litres chicken stock

To fry the cheeks

200g plain flour

4 eggs, whisked

250g panko breadcrumbs

rapeseed or sunflower oil, for shallow-frying

Preheat the oven to 170–180°C.

In a hot sauté pan or frying pan with a drizzle of oil, caramelize the cheeks, seasoning them, until browned all over, and remove to a plate. Add the vegetables and herbs to the pan and cook on a medium heat until really soft – they will deglaze the meat cooking juices. Add the red wine and reduce by almost three-quarters. Add the chicken stock and bring to the boil, then put the cheeks back into the pan – they should be swimming in the liquid. Turn off the heat, cover with foil and cook in the oven for 40–45 minutes, until the cheeks are very soft.

Remove the cheeks to a tray or plate and leave to cool to room temperature (if they are still hot, they will break up when you touch them).

While the cheeks are cooling, pass their cooking liquid through a sieve – press the vegetables down in the sieve with the back of a spoon, then discard. Ladle off as much of the fat that has risen to the surface as possible. Return to the heat and reduce until you have a gravy-like consistency. Keep warm.

For the salad

50g lovage leaves (or turnip tops or rocket – something flavourful)

1 bunch of fresh flat-leaf parsley, leaves picked

leaves from 1 head of celery

1 red onion, julienned

15ml Moscatel vinegar

30ml extra virgin olive oil

sea salt and freshly ground black pepper

Combine the salad leaves and red onion together so they are ready to dress at the last minute.

Coat the cheeks first with the flour, then with the whisked egg, then with the panko crumbs. Heat some oil in a high-sided pan or sauté pan on a medium heat and, when hot, shallow-fry the pig's cheeks until golden brown. Remove, and drain on kitchen paper.

When you are ready to serve, make a dressing for the salad by mixing the vinegar, olive oil, salt and pepper together. Drizzle the dressing over the salad and serve with the pig's cheeks, with the gravy in a little ramekin or bowl on the side for dipping.

CRISPY PIG'S EARS WITH *TXIMITXURRI* SAUCE
FOR 4 (2 SMALL EARS PER PERSON)

The word 'ears' in a recipe may not sound immediately appealing, but people are always (pleasantly!) surprised when they eat them for the first time: they are so soft and delicious – and simple and cheap. I normally use suckling pig's ears for this recipe, as they're smaller and more gelatinous. They can be difficult to get hold of, though, so if you can't find them just ask your butcher for the smallest possible pig's ears.

Tximitxurri is an Argentinian sauce, also known as *chimichurri*.

8 small or 4 medium-sized pig's ears

1 carrot, roughly chopped

1 leek, roughly chopped

2 sticks of celery, roughly chopped

1 onion, roughly chopped

1 bay leaf

½ a bunch of fresh thyme

¼ of a bunch of fresh sage

pomace or light olive oil, for shallow-frying

sea salt and freshly ground black pepper

2 tablespoons chopped fresh flat-leaf parsley leaves, to finish

For the *tximitxurri* sauce

2 shallots, finely chopped

50ml extra virgin olive oil

1 clove of garlic, finely chopped

25ml sherry vinegar

1 tablespoon chopped fresh flat-leaf parsley

1 tablespoon each of finely chopped fresh rosemary leaves, thyme, chives and tarragon

sea salt and freshly ground black pepper

Preheat the oven to 180°C.

Clean the ears very well, inside and out. Blowtorch the hair or burn it off over a gas flame. Wash thoroughly.

To cook the ears, put them into a roasting tray with the vegetables and herbs and enough water to cover them. Cover with foil and cook in the oven until very soft: the more tender the ears become, the more gelatinous they will be. The exact cooking time will depend on the size of the ears – but it will be around 40 minutes. To check whether they are done, remove the foil and poke them gently with a toothpick. Remove the ears from the tray, discarding the vegetables and liquid, and leave to cool.

While the ears are cooking, prepare the sauce: mix all the ingredients together and set aside.

When the ears are still warm, pour some olive oil into a pan and put on a medium heat. When it is hot, add the ears and season. Fry until golden brown – you want the skin to be as crispy as possible.

Eat the ears when they are still hot. Keep whole if small, or slice into three or four pieces if larger, and drizzle over the sauce. Sprinkle with the finely chopped parsley, and serve.

LAMB'S KIDNEYS, CHORIZO, GARLIC & PARSLEY CRUMBLE

FOR 4

This recipe is a great way of encouraging people to eat more offal, as the crumble adds a different texture, plus it's a very quick meal to prepare and cook and it's cheap and delicious. It's the kind of thing I eat when I want to feel warm and cosy.

Instead of lamb's kidneys, you could use veal kidneys, which have a less pronounced offal flavour.

12 cleaned lamb's kidneys with no fat, cut into cubes

25ml extra virgin olive oil

40ml Alameda or Oloroso sherry

100g chorizo, diced to half the size of the kidney cubes

3 teaspoons chopped fresh flat-leaf parsley leaves

2 cloves of garlic, chopped

120g panko breadcrumbs

sea salt and freshly ground black pepper

Preheat the oven to 180–200°C.

Fry the kidney cubes in a very hot pan with the olive oil. When they are caramelized, add the sherry.

Put the chorizo on a baking tray and place in the oven until caramelized – a couple of minutes. Then add the parsley, garlic, panko, salt and pepper to the tray, mix together and return to the oven (add a little bit more oil if you need) until the panko becomes golden brown – check after a couple of minutes.

Put the caramelized kidneys on plates, then cover completely with the crumble mix and serve: you should eat this with a spoon for scooping it up.

PENCAS

This is a really old recipe that my grandmother, who was a very good cook, taught to my mum. It's sort of like a sandwich, but made up of vegetables, Tetilla (a Galician cow's cheese), and a little bit of air-dried meat. Making it is a long process but it's so worth it when you eat it.

800g Swiss chard

2 teaspoons chilli oil (see page 284)

1 tablespoon ajillo (see page 283)

sea salt and freshly ground black pepper

400g Tetilla cheese

200g *cecina* (dried beef), thinly sliced

200g plain flour

4 eggs, whisked

250g panko breadcrumbs

rapeseed or sunflower oil, for shallow-frying

Separate the white stalks of the chard from the green leaves. Remove any stringy bits from the stalks. Blanch the green leaves in boiling salted water until very soft, then remove to iced water. Next, blanch the white stalks until very soft. Chop the stalks into little rectangles around 6cm x 4cm. Chop the green leaves finely.

Add the chilli oil and *ajillo* to the chopped greens, season with salt and pepper and mix together.

Cut the cheese into ½cm thick slices the same size as the chard stalks.

Add some chopped greens to a square of white chard stalk. Top with a thin slice of *cecina*, then a slice of cheese, then another slice of *cecina*, then more greens, then another piece of chard stalk.

Squish together, then coat in flour, egg and panko.

Put a couple of centimetres of oil into a high-sided pan or sauté pan on a medium-low heat and shallow-fry – you don't want to colour the *pencas* too much, but you want to cook them until the cheese melts.

Drain on kitchen paper, then cut in half diagonally, so you can see all the layers, and season.

EGGS

Every time I go home to see my family, my mum asks, 'What do you fancy today – fried eggs and peppers?' And I always say yes.

In Spain, if you open most people's fridges, you'll see that the tray for holding eggs is completely full – generally, people don't just have half a dozen. Eggs are really important in Spanish cooking: we love them boiled and fried (poached, not so much), and you need to have a good stash to hand in order to make tortillas, salads (see Russian salad, page 63) and lots of crispy fried eggs. I never eat fried eggs with a knife and fork: instead of cutlery, I have two pieces of bread – it's the most fun part of eating them. I always finish them off with a little olive oil, Moscatel vinegar and sweet smoked paprika, for that extra bit of flavour. Eggs make the quickest dinner and, unlike in the UK where they seem to be largely considered a breakfast food, dinnertime is generally when they are eaten in Spain.

Eggs and potatoes are often used together in Spanish cooking. They're two ingredients that people tend to always have lying around, so it makes sense. They pair wonderfully in salads (see the baby potato, ham, egg and tarragon salad, page 84), though the most famous egg and potato combination is, of course, the tortilla. When we were shooting the photos for this book, we stopped at this place at 8 a.m., after driving for an hour. We ordered coffees, and from where I was sitting I could see the woman who had served us in the small kitchen, making a tortilla. How could we resist? I love to eat tortilla hot, which is why I always cook mine so that it's runny, and this was fresh out of the pan. With a small piece of bread and a coffee it was heaven: the best breakfast you could ever have. When it comes to tortilla, you can eat it any time – it's something you never get bored with.

TORTILLA with *MORCILLA* & *PIQUILLO* PEPPERS

I ate this recently in Bilbao, at a bar in the medieval old town, or the Seven Streets, as it's known. You can't help but get lost there, and it's hopeless to try to retrace your steps – though you always stumble across somewhere new. This is a classic Basque way to eat tortilla and something people often make at home; we love to add extra flavours to our tortillas, and the earthiness of the *morcilla* with sweet *piquillo* peppers is amazing.

4 tablespoons extra virgin olive oil, plus enough to cook the potatoes

3 onions, julienned

sea salt and freshly ground black pepper

4 medium potatoes, peeled, halved lengthways, then cut into 3mm slices (a mandolin is useful here)

6 medium eggs

200g *piquillo* peppers, julienned

200g rice *morcilla* (Spanish black pudding), skin removed, meat crumbled

Put 2 tablespoons of oil into a pan on a low heat, then add the onions with a pinch of salt. Caramelize the onions very slowly until they are dark golden brown. Exactly how long this will take will depend on your pan, but you can't rush it – around 30 minutes.

Put at least 3cm of oil into another large non-stick pan on a low-medium heat. Season the sliced potatoes on the chopping board and add to the pan: don't overcrowd it, cook them in two batches if you need to. Cook until they start to get slightly soft and golden – you don't want 'fried' potatoes. Remove to a bowl or plate using a spider or a slotted spoon, and cook the second batch, if necessary.

It's important to make the tortilla mix while the onions and potatoes are still warm, as this will give your tortilla better flavour (make sure it's not hot, though: you don't want scrambled eggs!). First, mix the cooked onions and potatoes together, then whisk the eggs and add to the potato/onion mix. Add the chopped *piquillo* peppers and the crumbled *morcilla* and mix again. Leave to sit for at least 10–15 minutes. The potatoes will start to absorb the egg, and their juices will mix together.

Put 2 tablespoons of olive oil into a medium-sized pan that's 4cm deep, and put on a medium heat. When it starts to get warm, pour in the tortilla mix, and reduce the heat to low. You will see the edge of the tortilla start to set: this is when it's ready to turn.

Try to get a plate just slightly bigger than your pan – or use your pan lid if it has no rim. It's best to turn the tortilla off the heat: hold the pan close to you, place the plate on top, then confidently, in one smooth move, turn it over. Bring the plate close to the pan and carefully slide the tortilla back in, using a wooden spoon to nudge it into place if you need to. It's not easy – but you'll get better with practice.

Turn the heat back on and leave the tortilla to cook for another couple of minutes, then turn again, using the same method but cleaning your plate or lid first. I normally turn a tortilla three times, so it develops as minimal a crust as possible. You can check how cooked your tortilla is by poking it with a toothpick. Some people like it well done but I like it nice and juicy. You can also press it with your finger: if it rises up at the sides, it is still too eggy. When it is done, turn it out a final time and leave to rest for 10 minutes before slicing.

Serve sliced, with a crispy salad (such as Little Gem) on the side. Refrigerate any leftover tortilla and take it out of the fridge for an hour or so before eating.

EGGS

TORTILLA WITH CHORIZO FOR 4

A tortilla welcomes anything, so you can be adventurous with what you add to the basic potato and onion mix: peppers, asparagus, leftover roast vegetables . . . I like to eat it hot, but some people prefer to eat it the day after. The best is when you come home at 3 a.m. to a slice of leftover tortilla.

You want to use potatoes that are very yellow inside: I like Maris Piper. The ideal ratio should be 70% potatoes to 30% onions.

Making a tortilla is a long journey, and although the final cooking is quick, you will need to be well organized and have lots of pans on hand.

4–5 table-spoons extra virgin olive oil, plus enough to cook the potatoes

3 onions, julienned

sea salt and freshly ground black pepper

4 medium potatoes, peeled, halved lengthways, then cut into 3mm slices (a mandolin is useful here)

6 medium eggs

200g good-quality cooking chorizo, cut into approx. 2cm x 2cm cubes

alioli (see page 287), to serve

Put 2 tablespoons of oil into a pan on a low heat, then add the onions with a pinch of salt. Caramelize the onions very slowly until they are dark golden brown. Exactly how long this will take will depend on your pan, but you can't rush it – around 30 minutes.

Put at least 3cm of oil into another large non-stick pan on a low-medium heat. Season the sliced potatoes on the chopping board and add to the pan of oil: don't overcrowd it – cook them in two batches if you need to. Cook until they start to get slightly soft and golden – you don't want fried potatoes. Remove to a bowl or plate using a spider or a slotted spoon, and cook the second batch, if necessary.

It's important to make the tortilla mix while the onions and potatoes are still warm, as this will give your tortilla better flavour (make sure it's not hot, though: you don't want scrambled eggs!). First, mix the cooked onions and potatoes together, then whisk the eggs and add to the potato/onion mix. Leave to sit for at least 10–15 minutes. The potatoes will start to absorb the egg, and their juices will mix together.

Put a drizzle of olive oil into a pan on a medium heat and fry the chorizo until slightly crisp on the outside but still juicy inside. Take off the heat, leave for a minute, then add the chorizo and its cooking juices to the tortilla mix. Mix together.

Put 2 tablespoons of olive oil into a medium-sized pan about 4cm deep, and place on a medium heat. When it starts to get warm, pour in the tortilla mix, and reduce the heat to low. You will see the edge of the tortilla start to set: this is when it's ready to turn.

Try to get a plate just slightly bigger than your pan – or use your pan lid if it has no rim. It's best to turn the tortilla off the heat: hold the pan close to you, place the plate on top, then confidently, in one smooth move, turn it over. Bring the plate close to the pan and carefully slide the tortilla back in, using a wooden spoon to nudge it into place if you need to. It's not easy – but you'll get better with practice.

Turn the heat back on and leave the tortilla to cook for another couple of minutes, then turn again, using the same method but cleaning your plate or lid first. I normally turn a tortilla three times, so it develops as minimal a crust as possible. You can check how cooked your tortilla is by poking it with a toothpick. Some people like it well done but I like it nice and juicy. You can also press it with your finger: if it rises up at the sides, it is still too eggy. When it is done, turn it out a final time and leave to rest for 10 minutes before slicing.

Serve sliced, with the *alioli* on top and a nice piece of bread and some salad leaves – like Little Gem – on the side. Refrigerate any leftover tortilla and take it out of the fridge for an hour or so before eating.

SPANISH POTATO SALAD

This is a typical dish from Cádiz that's served cold. Every time I am in the south I have this salad because it's so fresh-tasting, and it's something I grew up with too: everyone eats *papas alinadas* at home. As a child, I loved dipping a piece of bread into the juices you're left with at the end. I still do.

sea salt and freshly ground black pepper

4 good-quality yellow waxy potatoes, of similar size

4 eggs

½ a red onion

20 fresh flat-leaf parsley leaves

200g tinned *ventresca* (belly) tuna, drained

75ml extra virgin olive oil

20ml Moscatel vinegar

Fill a pan with cold water and add a pinch of salt. Add the potatoes and bring to a gentle boil (if the water is bubbling too much it will break up the potatoes). Cook until very soft, then remove with a slotted spoon to a colander to drain – if you pour them out they will break up. While they are still warm, peel the potatoes with a small knife and cut into roughly 3cm chunks.

Fill a smaller pan with water and bring to the boil. When it's bubbling, add the eggs and boil for 10 minutes, then drain and peel them under running water (it's easier to peel them this way). Cut them into quarters.

Slice the onion very thinly into julienne. Roughly slice the parsley leaves – don't chop them, you want to eat them as part of the salad.

Put the potatoes on a platter, and top with layers of egg, onion, parsley and tuna.

Cover and refrigerate for around 20 minutes, or until it's nice and cold. When you're ready to eat, drizzle over the olive oil and vinegar and season with salt and pepper. Serve with bread, to scoop up the juices.

JERUSALEM ARTICHOKE PURÉE, FRIED EGG & TRUFFLE

FOR 4

If you're lucky enough to have a white truffle, use that. Otherwise, you can use a summer or winter truffle, or even jarred truffles. We call these fried eggs *puntillas*, meaning 'lacy', because of their crispy edges.

For the Jerusalem artichoke purée

500g Jerusalem artichokes

125ml whole milk

2 bay leaves

25ml extra virgin olive oil, for frying, plus 40ml for blending

3 cloves of garlic, thinly sliced

3 shallots, chopped

100g *jamón*, roughly chopped

1 litre chicken stock

sea salt and freshly ground black pepper

For the fried eggs

rapeseed oil – enough to fill your pan to 1cm

4 eggs

1 tablespoon extra virgin olive oil, to finish

sea salt and freshly ground black pepper

To finish

truffle (white, summer or winter)

Peel the Jerusalem artichokes, putting the peeled roots into a bowl with the milk and enough water to cover them – this stops them discolouring. Pour into a pan (top up the water, if necessary), add the bay leaves and boil until soft, then drain and rinse.

Put the 25ml of olive oil into a pan on a medium-low heat and gently fry the garlic, shallots and *jamón* – you don't want them to colour. Add the chicken stock and cook until it reduces by half, then add the artichokes, season, and continue to cook. When there is hardly any liquid in the pan and almost all the stock has been absorbed by the artichokes, the mixture is ready to blend. Add the additional 40ml of olive oil when blending, to emulsify – this gives the purée a creamier texture. Transfer to a saucepan and keep warm.

Put 1cm of oil into a pan on a medium heat, and crack in the eggs, 2 at a time. Fry until they are crispy at the edges – I like to spoon some of the hot oil over the yolks, so that they cook slightly but are still runny inside. I also lift up the white around the yolks four times so that the oil can better cook it. When the eggs are golden and crispy at the edges, remove them with a slotted spoon to a paper-lined plate. Season with a tablespoon of olive oil, salt and pepper, then cook the next 2 eggs in the same way.

Put the artichoke purée on plates, top with the eggs and shave over the truffle, using a truffle mandoline or the small, lumpy side of a grater. Serve with good bread.

BROKEN EGGS, PEPPERS & POTATOES

FOR 2

This recipe is exactly what you need when you're hungover: it's very naughty. Ideally, after eating it, you'd go straight back to bed.

2 large potatoes

2 long red peppers

½ an onion

3 tablespoons extra virgin olive oil, plus enough to cook the potatoes and eggs

sea salt and freshly ground black pepper

1 bay leaf

4 eggs

1 tablespoon smoked paprika

20ml Moscatel vinegar

Peel the potatoes and chop into chip-size pieces (don't waste any potato trying to make them too perfect, though). Wash the peppers, then halve, deseed and cut into 1cm strips – similar in size to the potatoes. Cut the onion to the same sort of size.

Into a high-sided sauté pan or similar, on a medium-low heat, put enough olive oil to just cover the potatoes (around 2cm). Fry them until golden brown (roughly 5–6 minutes) – you don't want them to get crispy. Remove the potatoes and set aside. Add another tablespoon of olive oil to the same pan on a medium heat. Add the onions, with some salt and pepper and the bay leaf, and fry until very soft and slightly coloured. Add the peppers and continue cooking until caramelized, then add the potatoes and remove the bay leaf. The potatoes should soak up all the juices in the pan. Don't mix with a spoon, as it will break the potatoes up, but give the pan a shake to fold everything together. Season and take off the heat.

Put 1cm of olive oil into a pan on a medium heat and crack in the eggs, 2 at a time. Fry until they are crispy at the edges – I like to spoon some of the hot oil over the yolk, so that it cooks slightly but is still runny inside. I also lift up the white around the yolk four times so that the oil can better cook it. When the eggs are golden and crispy at the edges, remove them with a slotted spoon to a paper-lined plate. Season with a tablespoon of olive oil, and some salt and pepper, then cook the next 2 eggs in the same way.

Place the eggs on top of the potatoes, onions and peppers. Drizzle over a final tablespoon of oil, then season with salt and pepper, smoked paprika and vinegar. Slice across the eggs so that they are 'broken'.

BABY POTATO, HAM, EGG & TARRAGON SALAD

FOR 4–6

This is nice for breakfast or a quick early dinner.

800g baby potatoes

sea salt and freshly ground black pepper

1 bay leaf

6 eggs

70ml extra virgin olive oil

4 shallots, chopped

6 thin slices of Ibérico or Serrano ham, yellow fat trimmed, cut into finger-sized strips

½ a bunch of fresh tarragon, chopped

Put the potatoes into a pan with plenty of salted water and a bay leaf. Bring to the boil and cook until the potatoes are nice and soft. Gently drain, then cut the potatoes in half.

Put the eggs into a pan of boiling water and cook for 7 minutes, then remove them to a bowl of cold water.

Put 50ml of olive oil into a pan on a medium heat. Add the potatoes and cook until golden brown and caramelized. Add the shallots and cook gently, then add the ham for a couple of minutes – you don't want it to crisp, just to lose its saltiness slightly. Stir in the tarragon.

Put the potatoes on a plate. Cut the boiled eggs into quarters and dot over the potatoes, then finish with the remaining olive oil, salt and pepper.

CONSOMMÉ WITH POACHED EGG

FOR 4

This is all about clean flavours. In Spain, when it's very cold, it's common to have a '*caldo*' (consommé stock) in the kind of bar where you go to have a small beer or a coffee. It comes steaming, like a cup of tea – consommé should always be served very hot.

4 duck eggs

extra virgin olive oil, for drizzling

smoked paprika, for sprinkling

For the consommé

3 egg whites

For the stock

2 medium Spanish onions, peeled and cut in half

1 oxtail

1 beef knee joint

1 good-quality chicken leg

2 pieces of *jamón ibérico* bone

200g dried chickpeas, soaked overnight in cold water

300ml white wine

¼ of a bunch of fresh flat-leaf parsley, tied together with string

1 bay leaf

3 leeks, white part only, tied together

3 carrots, peeled

1 whole head of garlic

First make the stock. Put the 4 onion halves into a pan on a medium-low heat with no oil and burn the cut side of the onions until black – this will take about 20 minutes.

Put all the meat into a very large pan, cover with cold water and bring to the boil. Simmer for 10–12 minutes – all the impurities will rise to the surface. Drain, then rinse the meat and the pan. Return the meat to the pan and cover with 5 litres of fresh water. Wrap the chickpeas in muslin, tie together and add to the pan. Add the wine.

Tie the parsley and bay together. Tie the leeks and carrots together separately. Add to the pot with the garlic, cut in half horizontally, and the burnt onions. There should be enough space for everything to float. Cook very gently on a low heat for 3 hours minimum.

Remove the meat from the pot, and the vegetables separately. The garlic, parsley, bay leaf, beef knee joint, ham bones and onions can be discarded. Next, you need to strain the stock through some muslin. The simplest way to do this is to tie the muslin over the top of a clean saucepan – make sure you leave enough slack so that it doesn't buckle. Gently pour the stock through the muslin and set aside to cool.

Pick the meat off the bones. Chop the vegetables into small cubes.

Put 500ml of the cooled stock into a bowl with the egg whites and whisk together. Pour back into the pan of stock, stir a little, then leave it alone! Put the pan on a very low heat: you need it to be really gentle or the egg whites will start to cook. The egg whites will start to rise and form a crust, bringing all the impurities up with them – when the stock reaches this point, it's ready. Carefully remove the crust with a ladle.

Gently pour the stock through the muslin again – you should now have a clear stock. For 4 people, you will need around 800ml of stock, but you can freeze any extra for use another time.

Fill a saucepan with water and bring to the boil. Add vinegar and salt. Crack a duck egg into a small ramekin or glass, then gently pour the egg into the boiling water and poach for 1½–2 minutes. Remove to a plate with a slotted spoon and repeat until you have poached all the eggs. Drizzle over a little olive oil and sprinkle with smoked paprika.

Warm up the stock. Divide the vegetables and meat between four bowls, then pour over the stock, add a semi-poached egg to each bowl, and leave for 30–40 seconds to continue cooking before serving.

IBERIAN SCOTCH EGGS

I first ate a Scotch egg in a gastropub in England. I thought, 'What is that?' Then I cut into it and I saw the runny yolk . . . I wondered why I'd never had anything similar in Spain, as we love eggs so much, and then I thought that it would be a good idea to make a Scotch egg using Iberian pork – it has so much flavour.

If you pre-boil your eggs, make sure you leave them to come back to room temperature before wrapping and frying.

6 medium eggs

150g plain flour

3 eggs, whisked

150g panko breadcrumbs

rapeseed or sunflower oil, for frying

extra virgin olive oil, to finish

For the mince

500g Iberian pork mince (80% meat, 20% fat)

sea salt and freshly ground black pepper

2 cloves of garlic, crushed

4 tablespoons chopped fresh flat-leaf parsley leaves

½ teaspoon cayenne pepper

1 teaspoon smoked paprika

Put the eggs into a pan of boiling water and cook for 6½ minutes, then remove to a bowl of ice-cold water. When cool enough to handle, peel off the shells.

Mix all the mince ingredients together.

Lay one-sixth of the mince mixture on a piece of cling film 15cm x 15cm, put an egg in the middle, then pull the cling film around it – this helps the meat to cover the egg evenly without falling apart. You want a layer of around 1cm. Repeat with the rest of the eggs. Dip in flour, then egg, then panko.

Preheat the oven to 180°C.

Pour oil into a large high-sided pan – you want enough to come halfway up the eggs – and put on a medium-low heat. When hot (but not too hot, as you don't want the panko to burn), shallow-fry the Scotch eggs, turning them until they are golden on all sides. Drain them on a baking tray lined with kitchen paper, then remove the paper and finish cooking the eggs in the oven for 4–6 minutes, to ensure that they are cooked through and hot inside. To check that the eggs are cooked, stick a toothpick inside one for 20 seconds, then raise it to your lips (don't burn yourself) – if the toothpick is warm, the eggs are done.

Serve the Scotch eggs cut in half and seasoned with a little olive oil, salt and pepper.

SCRAMBLED EGGS, WILD MUSHROOMS, PRAWNS & *PIQUILLO* PEPPERS

FOR 4

This is ideal for breakfast or brunch, but would also make a perfect tapa or *pintxo* – just cook the eggs a little longer so they're not so runny.

200g girolles and ceps

50ml extra virgin olive oil

sea salt and freshly ground black pepper

2 shallots, finely diced

2 cloves of garlic, finely sliced

4 *piquillo* peppers, seeds removed, julienned

12 regular-size raw prawns, peeled and deveined

8 eggs, whisked (do not season, as this will make the eggs watery)

4 teaspoons chopped fresh flat-leaf parsley leaves

Clean the mushrooms to get rid of any dirt or grit: some people use a brush, but I think the best way is to dab them carefully with a J-cloth. Leave the girolles whole and cut the ceps into 4-5 thin slices (so that they are the same size as the girolles).

Put the oil into a large pan on a medium heat and cook the girolles first, to cook off their water. Season the girolles, then add the ceps and let them caramelize a little (1–1½ minutes), then add the shallots and garlic. Cook gently for a couple of minutes, lowering the heat slightly to medium-low, then add the *piquillos*. Cook for a minute, just to bring everything together, then add the prawns and season again.

When the prawns are halfway cooked, add the whisked eggs and turn the heat up to medium-high. Leave for a second, then stir a little, leave again, then stir again – and repeat. The eggs are done when you can see that they are shiny but not liquid. Remember that they will continue to cook when you take them off the heat. Sprinkle over the parsley and serve with toast.

MIGAS

This old Spanish recipe transforms old bread into a hot, filling meal. The bread is first soaked and then toasted, taking on the juice and oil of whatever else you have around and have added to the pan. There are many different variations, but classically it's peasant or wartime food; *migas* means 'crumbs'. My mum's version is different from this recipe: she would always sit shaving the bread into a large bucket on the floor while chatting and catching up with family. *Migas* is the kind of thing you make for a feast where you're feeding at least 10–12 people. This recipe is for a more manageable serving size, and I like to cut the bread into chunks rather than shaving it.

400g stale bread (or frozen bread), cut into 2cm-ish cubes

125ml whole milk

3 tablespoons extra virgin olive oil, plus enough to cook the eggs

50g chorizo, diced

1 large long red pepper, diced

2 shallots, chopped

2 teaspoons smoked sweet paprika

50g pine nuts, roasted for a couple of minutes

50g hazelnuts, roasted for a couple of minutes

60g *morcilla* (Spanish black pudding), cut into cubes

50ml Alameda or Oloroso sherry

sea salt and freshly ground black pepper

4 eggs

2 tablespoons fresh flat-leaf parsley leaves

Sprinkle water over the bread cubes to dampen them, then pour over the milk.

Put 2 tablespoons of olive oil into a wok on a medium-high heat. Working quickly, add the chorizo first. Let it caramelize and, when it releases its oil, add the peppers for a minute, then the shallots, paprika, pine nuts and hazelnuts. Next add the crumbled *morcilla*, then the sherry. Cook to evaporate the alcohol, then squeeze out the *migas* (the soaked bread) a little and add to the pan, moving everything around quickly to make sure nothing burns. Season with salt and pepper.

Pour 1cm of oil into a separate pan and put on a medium heat. Crack in the eggs, 2 at a time, and fry until they are crispy at the edges – I like to spoon some of the hot oil over the yolk, so that it cooks slightly but is still runny inside. I also lift up the white around the yolk four times so that the oil can better cook it. When the eggs are golden and crispy at the edges, remove with a slotted spoon to a paper-lined plate, then cook the next 2 eggs in the same way.

Put the crispy eggs on top of the *migas*, drizzle over a tablespoon of olive oil and scatter over the parsley leaves. Season with salt and pepper and cut the eggs up so the yolk runs over everything.

SALADS

In Spain there's always a salad on the table, but generally it follows a theme: iceberg or cos lettuce, boiled egg, tuna, white asparagus . . . if you went to my mum's house you would have a variation on this salad, and if you went to someone else's house you'd be guaranteed to have something very similar again. It's a classic, and I love it, but I think it's fair to say that the table leans towards meat or fish rather than a range of different salads (the Russian salad on page 63, though traditional, can't really be classed as a salad).

It's probably for this reason that the salads in this chapter are inspired by what I've learned working in London over the last almost twenty years. Some chefs might think that making a salad isn't important, especially if it's served as a side. But it's just as important as cooking what you might consider a typical 'main' (i.e. meat or fish), and actually more challenging to make really well.

So what makes a great salad? For me, it's all about flavour (of course), colour and texture. By texture, I mean the crunch you get from biting down on vegetables, not leaves, and the juice that they release in your mouth. Although teeny little salad leaves look very beautiful, no sooner do you add dressing to them than they wilt. For this reason, the salads in this chapter are fairly low on leaves but big on vegetables.

The way you cut vegetables is so important to the texture of your salad, whether it's juicy wedges of tomato (see tomato, fennel and avocado salad, page 99) or crisp half-moons of fennel (see fennel, pear and radish salad, page 98). It's fashionable to grate and mandoline vegetables so that everything is very bitty or paper-thin: this looks beautiful but, as with little leaves, once you add olive oil or dressing that's it. To my mind, there's nothing worse than an attractive, crunchy salad without enough dressing. When I'm cutting into a piece of chicory (see chicory, anchovy and *salmorejo* salad, page 105), I want to be able to dip it in the dressing – this is what will make the flavours explode. A salad shouldn't be swimming in dressing, obviously, but you should be generous with it – it really does make all the difference.

PERSIMMON, GOAT'S CHEESE &
LAND CRESS SALAD

FOR 4

When persimmons are in season and ripe, this salad is so good and only takes 5 minutes. The best persimmons I've tried are from Sicily. Don't try to make this with hard persimmons – it's pointless. The goat's cheese should be creamy and very soft – you should almost be able to spread it.

I always keep a large piece of bread in the freezer: if you take it out and leave it for 20 minutes to thaw slightly, you will be able to slice it very thinly (this works best with bread that's not very wide).

This makes a great starter or light lunch or dinner.

8 sage leaves

60ml extra virgin olive oil, plus a little for the bread

around ¼ of a loaf (15cm) of frozen baguette or thin white bread, left for 20 minutes to defrost slightly

100g land cress (or something peppery like watercress or rocket)

4 very ripe persimmons

200g soft creamy goat's cheese

freshly ground black pepper

Preheat the oven to 160–170°C.

Put the sage leaves into a saucepan and just cover with olive oil, then put on a very low heat. As soon as the oil is warm, turn the heat off and leave to infuse, stirring gently. Discard the leaves.

Cut the partially defrosted bread into eight very thin slices. Place on a lined baking tray and drizzle with a little olive oil, then bake until the bread is crispy on both sides.

Place the salad leaves on a plate and put the toasts on top.

Cut the persimmons in half – they should be deep orange and really juicy – then cut into wedges as well as you can. Cut the goat's cheese to a similar size. Lift the persimmon halves carefully on to the toast slices and top with a slice of goat's cheese. Drizzle the sage-infused oil over the top and season with black pepper.

FENNEL, PEAR & RADISH SALAD

When I make salads like this, I like the ingredients to be crunchy and have some texture rather than being paper-thin, so I cut everything with a sharp knife instead of a mandoline – it doesn't matter if it's not perfect. You should be able to bite into the fennel so that it releases its juices in your mouth – almost like eating an apple. The pears should be sweet but not overly ripe.

2 fennel bulbs, with fronds

16 breakfast or heritage radishes

1 pear

½ a bunch of fresh dill

50ml extra virgin olive oil

25ml Moscatel vinegar

sea salt and freshly ground black pepper

Trim the top of the fennel (keep any fronds but discard the tops of the stalks). Cut in half, lengthways, on a slant. Then cut into 2mm half-moons, as though you are cutting an onion.

Keep the radish tops if they are very fresh and nice, otherwise trim them. Cut the radishes in half.

Peel the pear, cut in half, remove the core, then cut into 2mm half-moons, like the fennel.

Chop the dill finely.

Mix everything together with the olive oil, vinegar and salt and pepper, and serve straight away.

TOMATO, FENNEL & AVOCADO SALAD

FOR 4–6

I like a proper tomato salad: if you give me two or three pieces of tomato in a salad, I probably won't eat them. This salad is very colourful, with plenty of flavour. The tomatoes should be soft and ripe; like any fruit, you shouldn't keep them in the fridge. The dressing quantity is very generous, as you want to be able to mop it all up with the tomato and avocado. It's not the same as dressing a leaf salad – when things are crunchy they need olive oil.

60ml extra virgin olive oil

30ml sherry vinegar

sea salt and freshly ground black pepper

1kg mixed heritage tomatoes

2 fennel bulbs, with fronds

2 ripe avocados

18 fresh basil leaves

Put the olive oil, vinegar, salt and pepper into a jar with a lid and shake together.

Slice the tomatoes into 1cm thick wedges.

Trim the top of the fennel (keep any fronds but discard the tops of the stalks). Cut in half, lengthways, on a slant. Then slice into 3mm half-moons, as though you are cutting an onion. Cut the avocados in half and slice into thin half-moons, like the fennel.

Place two layers of tomatoes on your plate, then add the fennel and avocado. Pour the dressing over your salad and finish with the basil leaves, fennel fronds and some salt and pepper.

JUDIÓN & FENNEL SALAD
WITH SMOKED SALMON

FOR 4–6

The *judión* is a big, flat bean – similar to a butter bean. They are good in stews but are at their best in cold salads, as they are really creamy inside. You don't see this type of bean in many restaurants, but it is very Spanish. You can find *judiones* in Spanish delis and online, but you could also use any other dried flat white bean.

300g dried *judión* beans, soaked overnight (see method)

2 bay leaves

1 onion, cut in half

125ml extra virgin olive oil

60ml Moscatel vinegar

sea salt and freshly ground black pepper

2 fennel bulbs, diced

1 bunch of fresh dill, chopped

300g smoked salmon, sliced into thin strips

Put the *judión* beans into a large bowl (remember that they will expand) and cover with plenty of hot water. Leave to soak overnight.

The next day, drain the *judiones* and put into a pan with fresh cold water, the bay leaves and the onion. Place on a medium heat and bring to the boil, then reduce the heat and cook until nice and soft. Drain.

In a large bowl, whisk together the olive oil, vinegar, salt and pepper to make a dressing, then add the fennel, dill and drained beans and mix together. Spoon on to small plates, and top with the salmon.

BEETROOT SALAD WITH *AJO BLANCO* & DILL VINAIGRETTE

FOR 4–6

There are two types of people: those who hate beetroot and those who love it. People often don't like it because they think it's too earthy – but they tend not to have eaten a good beetroot. This salad is sweet; people who think they don't like beets love them when they try it. Ideally you should leave the *ajo blanco* ingredients to sit overnight, though you could leave them for just a couple of hours if you're pressed for time.

This goes especially well with fish.

1kg mixed baby beetroots, a combination of normal, golden, candy, white and the long, slim Cylindra variety (depending on what's in season and what you can find)

2 white peaches

½ a bunch of land cress, rocket or watercress, to finish

For the *ajo blanco*

½ a large loaf of white bread

80g whole blanched almonds

1 clove of garlic, crushed

300ml whole milk

50g seedless red grapes, cut in half

3 Granny Smith apples, peeled and cut into small chunks

25ml Moscatel vinegar

150ml extra virgin olive oil

sea salt and freshly ground black pepper

For the vinaigrette

1 bunch of fresh dill, very finely chopped

30ml Moscatel vinegar

90ml extra virgin olive oil

sea salt and freshly ground black pepper

First, make the *ajo blanco*. Put the bread, almonds, garlic and milk into a bowl, mix together and refrigerate overnight. The next day, put the contents of the bowl into a food processor with the grapes, apples and vinegar and blend until you have a creamy purée with no lumps. Add the olive oil and continue blending until creamy and fairly smooth, then adjust the seasoning to taste.

Put the unpeeled beetroots into a large pan of water with a pinch of salt and bring to a gentle boil. Cook until the beets are soft. Rather than checking this by piercing them with a knife (which makes the juices run out), remove a beetroot and squeeze both sides with your fingers: if you don't feel any resistance, they're done. Drain the beetroots and push the skin off with your hands while still warm. Cut into roughly 2½cm cubes (so you can eat them in one bite) and leave to cool.

Peel the peaches and cut into the same size cubes as the beetroot.

To make the dressing, put the chopped dill, vinegar and oil into a large bowl and whisk together to emulsify. Add the beetroot and peach cubes, then season with salt and pepper – seasoning at this stage makes it easier to see how much you need. Leave to sit for 5 minutes, mixing occasionally, so that the beetroots lose their juices slightly and mix with the dressing.

Spoon the *ajo blanco* on to your plates, followed by the dressed beetroot and peach, and top with the leaves.

CHICORY, ANCHOVY & SALMOREJO SALAD
FOR 4–6

Salmorejo and gazpacho are both cold soups from the south of Spain, but whereas gazpacho is made from cucumber, spring onions and peppers, *salmorejo* contains more bread, garlic and tomato, and is always finished with chopped hard-boiled egg and cubed *jamón*.

There is a lot going on in this fresh, crunchy salad – it's definitely not boring.

This salad goes brilliantly with lamb cutlets (see page 251) or pan-fried lamb sweetbreads (see page 252).

3 heads of yellow chicory, cut in quarters

8–12 good-quality anchovies

100g *jamón*, cut into cubes

1 bunch of watercress

2 hard-boiled eggs, chopped

For the dressing

40ml extra virgin olive oil

20ml Moscatel vinegar

sea salt and freshly ground black pepper

For the salmorejo

4 ripe tomatoes

¼ of a red pepper

2 cloves of garlic

50g bread, crusts removed

30ml sherry vinegar

125ml extra virgin olive oil

To make the *salmorejo*, put all the ingredients into a food processor or blender and blend to a creamy, gazpacho-like consistency.

Spoon the *salmorejo* on to a large platter or plate, place the chicory on top, and add an anchovy to each chicory quarter. Sprinkle over the cubes of *jamón*, the watercress and the chopped eggs.

To make the dressing, shake the oil, vinegar, salt and pepper together in a jar, and drizzle over the chicory.

Serve with large spoons for scooping up the chicory and *salmorejo*.

MOJAMA, AJO BLANCO & MANGO DRESSING

FOR 4–6

Mojama is air-dried tuna, made from the loin of the fish. It is very expensive because of the process involved in producing it – tuna costs a lot anyway, but *mojama* has to be salted, pressed and washed, then dried for 20–25 days. You can keep any leftover *mojama*, wrapped, in the fridge for a couple of weeks.

You want mangoes that are sweet and ripe (but not overly so) here. Mangoes aren't, of course, typical to Spain, but my mum always had some in the fruit basket when I was growing up.

Ideally you should leave the *ajo blanco* ingredients to sit overnight, though you could leave them for just a couple of hours if you're pressed for time.

250g *mojama*

2 Kent or Alphonso mangoes

For the dressing

30ml soy sauce

15ml sesame oil

1 fresh red chilli, very finely chopped

60ml extra virgin olive oil

juice of 1 lime

¼ of a bunch of fresh coriander, leaves picked, finely chopped

10g ginger, finely grated

¼ of a bunch of fresh dill, finely chopped

For the *ajo blanco*

½ a large loaf of white bread

80g whole blanched almonds

1 clove of garlic, crushed

300ml whole milk

50g seedless red grapes, cut in half

3 Granny Smith apples, peeled and cut into small chunks

25ml Moscatel vinegar

150ml extra virgin olive oil

sea salt and freshly ground black pepper

First, make the *ajo blanco*. Put the bread, almonds, garlic and milk into a bowl, mix together and refrigerate overnight. The next day, put the contents of the bowl into a food processor with the grapes, apples and vinegar and blend. Add the olive oil and continue blending until creamy and fairly smooth, then adjust the seasoning to taste.

Slice the *mojama* very thinly with a sharp knife – it doesn't have to be paper-thin.

To make the dressing, mix all the ingredients together.

Peel each mango and cut into small cubes: to do this, cut around either side of the stone, then turn and cut the other two sides, using a spoon to scoop out any extra flesh.

Spoon the *ajo blanco* on to your plates. Mix the mango cubes with the dressing and spoon on top, then add the *mojama*. Finish with a drizzle of olive oil, and season with a little pepper.

BABY VEGETABLE SALAD

Baby vegetables make an amazing, clean-tasting salad. This is great as a side to fish or meat and doesn't take long to prepare, as most of the vegetables should be al dente.

8 baby leeks, cleaned, cut widthways into 3 chunks

6 baby fennel, cut in half

8 baby turnips, peeled, leaves trimmed and washed

16 baby carrots, peeled

12 baby/young asparagus spears, ends snapped, kept whole or cut in half

1 tablespoon extra virgin olive oil

8 baby courgettes, trimmed

16 baby radishes, cleaned, leaves trimmed and washed

For the dressing

1 tablespoon fresh lemon thyme leaves

sea salt and freshly ground black pepper

60ml extra virgin olive oil

juice of 1 lemon

30ml Moscatel vinegar

To make the dressing, whisk all the ingredients together.

Fill a pan with water, add a pinch of salt and bring to the boil. Blanch the leeks until they are very soft and sweet – this should take a couple of minutes – then remove and set aside to drain. When the water is boiling again, blanch the fennel for 15 seconds, then remove and drain. Blanch the turnips for around 4 minutes, then remove and drain. Blanch the carrots until al dente. Finally, blanch the asparagus for 30–40 seconds and drain.

Put a tablespoon of olive oil into a pan over a medium heat and fry the courgettes for around a minute, until al dente with slightly caramelized skin.

Mix all the cooled vegetables together (including the uncooked radishes) with the leaves from the turnips and radishes if you have any, and add the dressing. Serve cold.

GEM SALAD WITH BOTTARGA, WALNUTS & PINE NUT DRESSING

FOR 4

The first Little Gem salad I put on a menu was with anchovies and smoked pancetta – it was a real hit but this has proved even more popular. Normally when you go to a restaurant you remember the fish or the meat, not the salad – but not in this case.

Wrap your leftover bottarga and keep it in the fridge. It's amazing added to rice with red mullet (see page 204) or grated over pasta.

3 Little Gem lettuces

50g pine nuts, roasted

3 shallots, finely chopped

½ a bunch of fresh chives, chopped

sea salt and freshly ground black pepper

50ml extra virgin olive oil

25ml Moscatel vinegar

45g Manchego cheese

4 whole fresh walnuts

1 bottarga (cured grey mullet roe)

Cut the Little Gems in half and trim the bottoms. Wash, then rinse and dry and put into a serving bowl.

Put the pine nuts, shallots and chives into a bowl, season and mix with the olive oil and vinegar. Pour over the Little Gem halves.

Using a fine grater, grate over the Manchego, the walnuts (they should be like snow), and finally the bright yellow bottarga.

CATALAN COD SALAD

FOR 4–6

This is a really fresh and easy salad. If you wanted to have it as a *pintxo*, you could thread the cod and tomato on to skewers or toothpicks and place them in Little Gem leaves.

Juicy tomatoes with a very thin skin are ideal for this. I think tomatoes should explode in your mouth and you don't get that when they're finely sliced, which is why I cut them into wedges. My dad used to cut up a tomato, season it with olive oil and salt and just bite into it . . . that's the way to eat tomatoes. Never put tomatoes in the fridge – if they are cold they won't taste of much.

3 really good-quality ripe, meaty tomatoes

sea salt

150g unpitted black Aragón olives

3 teaspoons capers

2 shallots, finely chopped

1 teaspoon chopped fresh tarragon

100ml extra virgin olive oil

30ml sherry vinegar

sea salt and white pepper

For the marinated salt cod

350g salt cod, desalinated for 24 hours (see method)

200ml extra virgin olive oil

plenty of white pepper

2 cloves of garlic, crushed to a paste

1 bunch of fresh flat-leaf parsley, leaves picked and roughly chopped

To desalinate the cod, rinse it, then place it in a container with plenty of water. You need to make sure the skin is facing up (if it's on the bottom the salt won't be released). Leave in the fridge for 24 hours, rinsing and changing the water three times in total.

Remove the salt cod from its final soak of water and dry with kitchen paper. Remove the skin and cut into bite-size pieces. Cover with the olive oil, pepper (salt isn't necessary here!), garlic and parsley and leave to marinate overnight.

Half an hour before you're ready to eat, take the salt cod from the fridge to give it time to come to room temperature.

Cut the tomatoes into wedges and put them on the plate you are going to serve the salad on. Season with salt, then top with the marinated cod pieces.

Just before eating (otherwise they will become mushy), pit the olives and mix with the capers, shallots, tarragon, olive oil, vinegar and a little white pepper. Scatter the olive dressing over the cod and tomatoes, and serve.

SALADS

OCTOPUS, PRAWN & VEGETABLE SALAD   FOR 6

The colours and flavours of this dish are stunning. But it doesn't matter how long or how gently you cook it, English octopus is always tough. You need to use double-sucker octopus (*Octopus vulgaris*) from Spain or Morocco: this is readily available and is always frozen. The freezing process breaks down the membranes, which actually makes the octopus softer. If you can't find octopus, you could use squid or cuttlefish instead.

Octopus is very important in Galicia. The old, traditional Galician way to cook it is in a giant handmade copper pot, which is supposed to give the octopus more flavour. This doesn't really happen any more, but it's not uncommon to add a few copper coins to the pan in homage to the old method, or to add a wine cork, which is said to soften the octopus. There are lots of different stories and methods!

12 regular-size raw prawns, peeled, deveined and cut into cubes

1 red onion, finely diced

1 green pepper, cut into 2cm cubes

1 red pepper, cut into 2cm cubes

1 fennel bulb, cut into 2cm cubes

2 fresh red chillies, chopped

2 tablespoons chopped fresh dill

200ml extra virgin olive oil

80ml sherry vinegar

sea salt and freshly ground black pepper

For the octopus

½ an onion, peeled

1 bay leaf

1 frozen octopus (approx. 2kg before defrosting), defrosted

To cook the octopus, fill a large pan with water, add the onion and bay leaf and put on a medium-high heat. When the water is steaming and close to boiling, take the octopus and (carefully) dip it into the water, then bring it up again – repeat three times. This makes the octopus relax, making the meat tender.

When the water starts to bubble again, lower the heat to low-medium and gently simmer the octopus according to its weight (20 minutes per kilo) – if the water is boiling too fast it will rip the octopus's skin, so adjust the heat accordingly.

Take a toothpick and jab it into the thickest part. If it goes through cleanly, with no resistance, it is cooked, but if it feels like there's something preventing you from pushing through, then it needs to cook for longer, otherwise it will be chewy. When you're happy it is cooked, carefully remove the octopus from the pan to a tray and leave to cool. Cut it into 2cm pieces.

Blanch the prawns for 40 seconds to 1 minute in boiling water, then use a slotted spoon to remove them to a bowl of iced water to stop them continuing to cook.

Mix together the vegetables, chillies, octopus, prawns and dill, add the olive oil, vinegar and salt and pepper to taste, and serve.

VEGETABLES

The longer I have been cooking, the more I have come to enjoy cooking vegetables. They are incredibly diverse and vary so much in flavour – much more so than, say, different types of fish. And you feel really good when you eat them: people are coming round to the fact that vegetables are a satisfying main course in themselves.

Peppers are perhaps the most important vegetable (though technically a fruit) in Spain, whether fresh, dried or jarred. Recently, I visited a market in Astigarraga, a village in Guipúzcoa, just a few miles from San Sebastián, and I could smell roasted peppers as soon as I got out of the car. I kept walking and finally came across this man with a machine roasting hundreds of peppers. Women came up to him and put in their orders for a kilo or five, before going off to finish their food shopping. They came back to pick up their peppers before taking them home to preserve. Basque cooking in particular uses a lot of green and red peppers, along with onions, so that as we cook, we see the white, red and green of the Ikurrina (Basque flag).

The most important thing to consider when cooking vegetables is making the most of what is in season, as everything tastes ten times better eaten then. Spring is when I go mad with fresh asparagus, beans and everything else (see green asparagus, *romesco* and Idiazabal cheese, page 138, and flat green bean, tomato and potato stew, page 125), but in summer there are peppers (see *escalivada*, page 137), autumn brings wild mushrooms (see wild mushroom rice, page 120) and roots, and winter, though less plentiful, produces very good cabbages (see braised Hispi cabbage with garlic cream sauce, page 122).

VEGETABLES

WILD MUSHROOM RICE

This is a creamy, slow-cooked rice. Wild mushrooms have so much flavour, especially in autumn when many varieties are in season, and are used a lot in Basque cooking. One very typical dish is pan-fried ceps finished with olive oil, chopped parsley, salt and pepper, with an egg yolk on top.

Though this recipe is simple, the mushrooms give the rice a real depth. The key here is making sure you cook the rice properly: I like it to be al dente, but if you prefer it with a little less bite, just add a splash more water and cook it for a bit longer – it won't dilute the flavour.

Don't be scared to wash the black trumpet mushrooms: it's the only way to clean them without ending up eating a load of dirt!

100g ceps

100g black trumpet mushrooms

100g girolles

60ml extra virgin olive oil

2 cloves of garlic, very finely chopped

4 banana shallots, finely chopped

sea salt and freshly ground black pepper

240g Calasparra rice

2 bay leaves

800ml chicken or vegetable stock

1 tablespoon fresh thyme leaves

To serve

Manchego cheese, shaved

fresh truffle (optional), shaved, as much as you like

Clean the mushrooms to get rid of any dirt or grit: some people use a brush, but I think the best way is to dab them carefully with a damp J-cloth. The exception to this is the black trumpets, which have a lot of mud inside them: put them in a colander under running water, then dry them gently on a cloth. Cut the ceps into ½cm slices, and leave the black trumpets and girolles whole (unless the latter are very large, in which case cut them in half).

Put the olive oil into a large shallow casserole dish or sauté pan on a medium heat, then add the ceps and cook for a minute. Add the girolles next, and cook for another minute, then finally add the black trumpets – these will lose a lot of water. When all the water has evaporated (you will be able to hear when this happens, as the mushrooms will start to sizzle as they cook), add the garlic and shallots and season a little. Cook for a minute or so, then add the rice and bay leaves and season again. Stir together and cook for a couple of minutes, continuing to stir with a spoon, to remove the starch from the rice.

Have your stock ready: you don't want it boiling or it will reduce (if it does, just top it up with water), but it should be steaming.

Lower the heat to a gentle medium-low and add a quarter of the stock to the pan, stirring with a spoon. When this evaporates, add more. Make sure the heat is medium-low, otherwise the stock will evaporate too fast, without cooking the rice. Continue doing this, stirring frequently, until you have used all the stock. Taste the rice, and when you're happy with its texture, sprinkle over the thyme and mix together.

Season again if necessary, and serve with shaved Manchego – if you're lucky enough to have a truffle, that makes a luxurious extra finishing touch.

BRAISED HISPI CABBAGE
with GARLIC CREAM SAUCE

FOR 4

This makes a lovely autumnal dinner – the way the cabbage is cooked means you have to cut into it in the same way you would a steak.

60g pine nuts

sea salt and freshly ground black pepper

2 Hispi cabbages, hard outer leaves removed

100ml extra virgin olive oil

2 shallots, very finely chopped

3 tablespoons chopped fresh flat-leaf parsley leaves

1 tablespoon smoked paprika

For the garlic cream sauce

250g garlic

300ml double cream

sea salt and freshly ground black pepper

150ml chicken or vegetable stock or water

To make the garlic cream sauce, halve the garlic cloves and remove the green middle section, if there is one. Roughly chop, put into a saucepan and cover with water. Bring to the boil, then rinse, add fresh water and bring to the boil again. Repeat this three times: the garlic should be soft and mild-tasting. Drain a final time, then pour over the cream, season and add the stock or water. Bring to the boil, season again, then blend until smooth.

Preheat your oven to 180°C. Roast the pine nuts for 30–40 seconds, until they are golden brown, then set aside.

Bring a large pan of salted water to the boil. Add the cabbages – if they're not too big, boil them whole, otherwise cut them in half. Remove to drain when they are soft (pierce with a toothpick to check). If whole, halve or quarter, depending on their size. Drizzle over about 40ml of olive oil and season.

Put 40ml of olive oil into a pan on a medium heat. Cook the cabbages until golden brown and caramelized on each side, adding more oil to the pan as necessary. Remove the cabbages from the pan.

Add 20ml of olive oil to the pan, lower the heat slightly, and cook the shallots gently for a couple of minutes. Add the pine nuts, and finally the parsley. Sprinkle the contents of the pan over the cabbages, and finish with smoked paprika.

FLAT GREEN BEAN,
TOMATO & POTATO STEW

FOR 4

This recipe reminds me of growing up and asking my mum, 'What's for lunch today?' Whenever she made it, I would always eat two plates, as I didn't want anything else.

The starch from the potatoes creates a sauce for the beans with the tomatoes, and the garlic sprinkled over at the end refreshes the stew.

1kg (unprepped weight) flat green (Romano) beans

3 large potatoes

65ml extra virgin olive oil

3 shallots, chopped

3 fresh plum tomatoes, skin on, chopped

1 bay leaf

125ml sherry or white wine

sea salt and freshly ground black pepper

3 cloves of garlic, sliced very thinly

20ml Moscatel vinegar

To prepare the beans, first clean them, then cut into the top of each bean and pull towards you to remove the stringy section down the side (if you have really good-quality, thin beans then you won't need to do this). Cut the beans into 4cm pieces.

Peel the potatoes. Partially cut into them, then pull them apart into chunky, uneven-edged pieces similar in size to the green beans. These potatoes are called 'cachelos'.

Put 40ml of olive oil into a pan on a medium heat and cook the shallots, then add the tomatoes and cook until paste-like, to make a *sofrito*. Add the potatoes, bay leaf and sherry or wine, and cook until the alcohol has evaporated. Add the green beans and enough water to cover everything, plus a little extra splash. Season with salt and pepper, then put the lid on and cook until the potatoes and beans are soft – around 20 minutes.

Put the remaining 25ml of olive oil into a separate pan on a low-medium heat, then add the garlic and cook until just golden brown – don't let it get too brown or it will taste bitter. Turn off the heat, add the vinegar and mix together. Sprinkle the garlic over the stew before serving.

CAULIFLOWER with SALTED ALMONDS, SHALLOT & CHILLI

FOR 4

This is great served with pig's cheeks if you don't go the breaded *empanados* route (see page 66). Adding milk to the cooking water is meant to stop your house smelling of boiled cauliflower!

1 large cauliflower

100ml whole milk

sea salt and freshly ground black pepper

100g Marcona salted almonds

50ml extra virgin olive oil, plus more for drizzling

3 shallots, finely chopped

1 dried red chilli, finely chopped

3 tablespoons finely chopped fresh flat-leaf parsley leaves

Trim the stalk from the cauliflower and separate the florets. Peel the stalk and cut into short, thin strips similar in size to the florets. Put 100ml of water into a pan with the milk and a pinch of salt and bring to a gentle boil, then blanch the cauliflower stalks and florets until al dente. Drain and, if you are cooking the cauliflower in advance, place in a bowl of cold water.

Roughly crack the salted almonds with the back of a knife on a chopping board.

Put the oil into a pan on a medium heat, then add the drained cauliflower and allow to caramelize slightly. Add the shallots and cook gently until soft, then add the chilli and the almonds and cook for a minute or so. Season (remember that the almonds are already salted), then add the parsley. Take off the heat, drizzle with a little olive oil and mix everything together.

CREAMY MASHED POTATO & CHARD

FOR 4–6

This is an ideal accompaniment to roast pork or cutlets, and to fish like sea bream, sea bass and red mullet.

Plunging the chard into cold water after blanching ensures that it keeps its colour – this isn't essential, but it's useful if you want to cook the chard in advance. It's important to mash the potatoes while they are hot, as this makes them creamier and less lumpy. Adding the 'three fats' as I call them (cream, butter, olive oil) helps with this too.

800g Swiss chard, washed

30ml extra virgin olive oil

2 cloves of garlic, crushed

1 fresh red chilli, very finely chopped

For the mashed potato

4 good-quality medium potatoes

sea salt and freshly ground black pepper

1 bay leaf

100ml double cream

50g salted butter

40ml extra virgin olive oil

For the gravy

25ml extra virgin olive oil

2 shallots, chopped

1 carrot, diced

1 leek, diced

1 stick of celery, diced

½ an onion, diced

2 bay leaves

1 sprig of fresh thyme

500ml red wine

1 litre beef stock

Peel the potatoes and cut into big chunks, then put them into a pan of cold salted water with the bay leaf and bring to the boil. When cooked through, drain and mash. While the potatoes are cooking, put the cream, butter and olive oil into another saucepan and put on a medium-low heat. Stir occasionally and when almost boiling, add the mashed potatoes and mix together with a whisk over a low heat. Taste for seasoning and creaminess. Always add the fats to the potato when warm – they mix together and absorb flavour better.

To make the gravy, put the olive oil into a pan and cook the vegetables very gently with the herbs until they are mushy – the softer they are, the sweeter they will become, which will give the gravy more flavour. Add the wine and cook until the alcohol has evaporated, then add the beef stock and cook until the gravy is sauce-like but not too thick or sticky. Press through a sieve into a small pan and keep warm on a low heat, with the lid on so it doesn't reduce any further.

Separate the stalks and leaves of the chard. Blanch the whole stalks in boiling water until soft (keeping them as whole as possible stops them losing flavour), then remove to a bowl of iced water. Blanch the leaves too, then add these to the iced water. Drain the chard, and chop the stalks into 3–4cm pieces. Put the olive oil into a pan on a low heat, add the chard, and fry with the crushed garlic and chilli for a couple of minutes. Season with salt and pepper.

Lay the chard on top of the mashed potato and pour the warmed gravy on top.

GRILLED COURGETTES WITH PARSNIP PURÉE & ROCKET PESTO

FOR 4–6

You can generally find courgettes in a range of different shapes and colours at food markets these days. Grilling courgettes is one of the easiest ways to cook them, as there's hardly any prep – you just wash, slice and grill them.

1kg mixed courgettes (round, yellow and trompetta – these are long, pale and somewhat curly, and have fewer seeds than regular courgettes)

40ml extra virgin olive oil, plus more for drizzling

sea salt and freshly ground black pepper

a pinch of smoked paprika

5 walnuts, grated

For the parsnip purée

400g parsnips

500ml double cream

30g unsalted butter

50ml extra virgin olive oil

1 bay leaf

sea salt and freshly ground black pepper

For the rocket pesto

100g wild rocket

2 bunches of fresh basil

1 clove of garlic, crushed

200g pine nuts

200ml extra virgin olive oil

250g Manchego cheese (or hard sheep's cheese), cut into rough chunks

sea salt and freshly ground black pepper

To make the purée, peel the parsnips and cut into small cubes. Put into a pan with the double cream, butter, olive oil, bay leaf, salt and pepper and simmer until they are very soft. Remove from the heat and blend together until nice and creamy, tasting for seasoning. Return to a low heat, cover and keep warm.

To make the pesto, blend together the rocket, basil, garlic, pine nuts and olive oil to make a smooth-ish green paste. Add the Manchego and pulse so that you have little chunks of cheese, then add salt and pepper and mix together.

Cook the courgettes last. Trim them, slice them in half lengthways, then halve them again widthways. If you have round courgettes, cut them into wedges of a similar size. Put the courgettes into a bowl and season with olive oil, salt and pepper. Grill the courgettes on the barbecue or in a pan – if using the latter, carefully place each slice in the pan and turn them when they are coloured but still with a bite to them. When they are caramelized on both sides, remove to a tray or plate and drizzle with olive oil.

To serve, spoon the warm parsnip purée on to plates, top with the grilled courgettes, then dot over the pesto. Gently sprinkle over the smoked paprika, and finish with more olive oil and the grated walnuts.

GRILLED LEEKS VINAIGRETTE

This is very Basque, and a good dish for summer barbecues. Leeks and peppers are both pretty easy to get hold of and this is a really great way to eat them: it's all about the contrast of warm and cold, sweet and sour.

6 medium leeks

sea salt and freshly ground black pepper

a drizzle of extra virgin olive oils

For the vinaigrette

½ a red onion, very finely chopped

½ a red pepper, very finely chopped

½ a long green pepper, very finely chopped

25ml sherry vinegar

60ml extra virgin olive oil

sea salt and freshly ground black pepper

Trim the roots of the leeks, remove the first couple of layers, then cut off the green ends: you want to keep only the white and light green parts. Clean the trimmed leeks thoroughly to get rid of any dirt. Bring a large pan of slightly salted water to the boil and blanch the leeks until soft, then remove them to a large bowl of iced water.

Drain the leeks. You can cook them outside on the barbecue or, if you are cooking inside on the stove and the leeks aren't too large, you can fry them whole in a pan with a little drizzle of olive oil until they are golden brown all over. Season them while they are still warm and cut into four or bite-sized pieces.

Mix all the vinaigrette ingredients together, pour over the warm leek pieces and serve.

ESCALIVADA

This is such a versatile recipe: you can eat it on a Saturday morning on a piece of toast, by itself as a salad (with bread, of course), or alongside grilled fish or meat. It's particularly good with lamb, especially if you add a couple of anchovies. It will keep for up to 3 days in the fridge if you want to make it in advance. It's important to use ripe, good-quality vegetables – I find that Spanish or Italian peppers are the best in terms of flavour. My mum always prepares this salad with her hands. It's key that everything should be very soft, and that you keep all the vegetable juices.

Whenever I roast peppers I keep their skins and juices and add them to olive oil. I heat the oil very gently, then drain it: you're left with the most amazing smoky, roast-pepper-infused olive oil. Drizzle it on top of meat, fish, eggs – anything and everything.

4 large fresh plum tomatoes

2 Spanish or Italian red peppers

2 aubergines, skin pricked with a knife

1 large onion, skin on

1 whole head of garlic

90ml extra virgin olive oil

sea salt and freshly ground black pepper

30ml Moscatel vinegar

4 tablespoons chopped fresh flat-leaf parsley leaves

½ a bunch of fresh thyme, leaves picked

Preheat the oven to 180°C. Roast or barbecue all the vegetables and garlic until they are charred and juicy. The tomatoes and peppers will cook the quickest; the onions will take twice as long to become soft and sweet.

When the tomatoes are soft and glazed-looking, chop them, including the skins. Set aside. When the skin of the red peppers has caramelized, remove them to a bowl, cover with cling film, and leave to steam. Peel while still warm, then slice in half, remove the seeds and cut lengthways into 3cm-ish strips. Keep the pepper juice and strain it in a sieve, pressing it through with the back of a spoon or ladle.

When the aubergines are completely soft, cut them in half and remove the flesh with a spoon. Dress with half the olive oil, salt and pepper and chop roughly. When the onion is really blackened, remove the skin and cut into thick strips, similar in size to the peppers.

Squeeze out 3 or 4 of the roast garlic cloves into a bowl. Add the pepper juices and any other veg-cooking juices, along with the remaining olive oil, vinegar and herbs, and whisk together.

In a large bowl, gently fold together the aubergine, tomatoes, onions, red peppers and garlic dressing, then serve.

GREEN ASPARAGUS, *ROMESCO* & IDIAZABAL CHEESE

FOR 4–6

I love this with a crispy fried egg (*puntilla*) on top, or shaved summer truffle. You may not need all the *romesco*, but it isn't possible to make a smaller amount in the blender. Any that's left over will be delicious with everything, and it keeps well in the fridge.

16 fresh medium-sized English asparagus spears, hard woody ends snapped off (usually the end 3–4cm)

sea salt and freshly ground black pepper

80g roasted hazelnuts, roughly crushed with the back of a knife

2 shallots, chopped

3 tablespoons Pedro Ximénez (PX) balsamic vinegar

6 tablespoons extra virgin olive oil, plus a bit extra for the griddle

80g Idiazabal cheese (see page 41), or other sheep's cheese

1 x *romesco* (see page 56)

½ a bunch of fresh basil leaves

Blanch the asparagus in boiling salted water for 40 seconds, then remove to a bowl of iced water to stop them cooking and keep them green.

Mix the crushed hazelnuts in a bowl with the shallots, vinegar and olive oil to make a dressing. Shave the Idiazabal.

Drizzle a little more olive oil on a large griddle pan and put on a medium heat, then add the blanched asparagus and season with salt and pepper. Cook for around a minute – just enough to caramelize slightly and warm through.

Spoon the *romesco* on to your plates, place the asparagus on top and drizzle over the hazelnut dressing. Finish with the Idiazabal, thinly sliced, another drizzle of olive oil and the basil leaves.

FISH
AND
SHELL
FISH

Santurtzi is famous for sardines. The women who used to sell them, the *sardineras*, sang a song, 'From Santurtzi to Bilbao' (*Desde Santurce a Bilbao*), which describes how the women would walk by the riverside to Bilbao, with their baskets of sardines on their heads. It's very well known in Spain and people like to sing it at parties when they're having a good time!

Whether it's the traditional sardines or octopus, cooking fish doesn't have to be complicated. In Santurtzi, there is a restaurant by the port called Mandanga: it's known for its fresh fish, which is cooked on the charcoal grills outside, looking out to sea. It's one of my favourite places. It makes the whole town smell of grilled fish and I love it – to me, it's the smell of summer and holidays and home. Mandanga has been run by the same family for three generations, and they really know what they're doing. Imanol Bóveda, the grandson of the original owner, who runs the restaurant now, is the best at what he does: the fish is grilled, then finished with olive oil, garlic and that's it. Done. Sardines, turbot, bream and octopus are always on the menu, but one of the reasons Mandanga is so popular is that it's open to everyone: you can go there and eat sardines and mackerel and spend €20, or you can have langoustines and butterflied bream and spend €300. Whatever you choose, it will be amazing.

In the same way, the recipes in this chapter should have something for everyone, ranging from the cheap (cockles with parsley, chilli and sherry, page 178) to the more extravagant (baked scallops with garlic and parsley breadcrumbs, page 164), and from the speedy (squid, puntarelle, tomatoes, anchovies and capers, page 142) to the leisurely (the celebratory feast that is the seafood stew, page 208).

SQUID, PUNTARELLE, TOMATOES, ANCHOVIES & CAPERS

FOR 4

If you can't find puntarelle you can use something peppery and bitter, like rocket. This is easy, quick to make, tasty and healthy. All you need to buy is squid, tomatoes and puntarelle – the rest of the ingredients should be in your cupboard.

100ml extra virgin olive oil

800g good-quality squid, including tentacles, or cuttlefish (ask your fishmonger to clean them for you)

sea salt

20ml Moscatel vinegar

12 tinned anchovies, roughly chopped

2 tablespoons capers

300g Datterini or other fresh baby plum tomatoes, cut in half

150g puntarelle

(see page 283) and chilli oil see page 284), to finish

Put 50ml of olive oil into a pan on a medium heat. Season the squid with salt and fry for around 1½ minutes on each side – you don't want it to colour too much or to get a crust, as this will make it tough and chewy.

Combine the remaining olive oil with the vinegar, chopped anchovies, capers, tomatoes and just a little bit of salt (as the anchovies and capers are already salty) and mix with the puntarelle.

Put the salad on a plate, top with the squid, and finish with a drizzle of *ajillo* and chilli oil.

SQUID & PRAWN FISHBALLS
WITH SAFFRON SAUCE

FOR 4

Meatballs are usually made with beef or pork, but using the same technique is a really nice way to cook fish too. Serve these with boiled white rice or bread – or both!

500g squid (ask your fishmonger to clean them for you), chopped very finely

300g good-quality raw prawns, peeled, deveined and chopped finely

a pinch of saffron

3 cloves of garlic, chopped and mashed with a little salt

40g fresh flat-leaf parsley leaves, finely chopped

2 fresh red chillies, finely chopped

150g crustless bread, soaked in milk for 1 hour

sea salt and freshly ground black pepper

6 eggs

150g plain flour

rapeseed or sunflower oil, for frying

For the saffron sauce

20ml extra virgin olive oil

1 onion, finely chopped

1 bay leaf

sea salt and freshly ground black pepper

1 tablespoon saffron

120ml dry white wine

500ml fish stock or prawn stock (see page 288)

Mix the squid and prawns with the saffron, garlic, all but a sprinkling of the parsley, the chillies and the bread (squeeze out the milk). The mixture should have a dumpling-like consistency. Season with salt and pepper. Add 2 eggs — do not whisk them, but mix them in with your hands. Leave to rest for a couple of hours in the fridge.

Now mould the mixture into 40g balls, coating them with flour to make them less sticky. Whisk the remaining 4 eggs in a bowl. Put a heavy-based frying pan on a medium heat and pour in 3cm of rapeseed or sunflower oil. When the oil is hot, dip the floured fishballs in the egg mix for a second, letting any excess drip off, then cook them for 1–1½ minutes, or until golden brown. Remove from the pan with a slotted spoon and drain on kitchen paper.

To make the saffron sauce, put the oil into a pan on a medium heat. Add the onions and bay leaf and season. Cook the onions until they start to caramelize and get a little colour, then add the saffron. Pour in the wine and cook to evaporate the alcohol, then add the stock and bring to the boil. Season with salt and pepper to taste. Whiz to a light sauce in a blender, then put back into the pan and add the fishballs. Cook until the fishballs are tender and the sauce is sticky. To finish, garnish with the reserved parsley.

SQUID *ENCEBOLLADO*

This is a classic Basque dish and one of my favourites – I always order it as a starter. It can also be made with tuna, cut into cubes and fried very quickly.

Encebollado means 'cooked with onions': we love to caramelize onions in Spain, and the only thing you need to do it well is time.

75ml extra virgin olive oil

2 large onions, julienned

sea salt and freshly ground black pepper

2 bay leaves

100ml white wine

500ml prawn stock (see page 288)

800g squid, including tentacles (ask your fishmonger to clean them for you), bodies scored in diamonds

3 tablespoons chopped fresh chives

Put 25ml of olive oil into a large pan on a medium heat. Add the onions, a pinch of salt (this helps the onions to lose water and therefore cook more quickly) and the bay leaves. Cook, stirring occasionally, until the onions are about three-quarters of the way to being caramelized: they should be light golden brown but translucent. The time the onions take to cook will depend on the size of the pan used.

Add the wine and cook to evaporate the alcohol, then add the stock and reduce by about half, just so everything comes together – you're looking for a nice sauce-y spoonful.

Put the remaining 50ml of olive oil into another pan on a medium-high heat, and add the squid. Season with salt and pepper, and cook for 1–1½ minutes on each side – the tentacles might only need a minute.

Remove the squid to a chopping board and cut into three or four 2–3cm rings. Add to the pan of caramelized onions, mixing together, and cook for a couple of minutes more on a very low heat, just to bring it together. Finish with chopped chives, and serve.

CHICKPEA & SQUID STEW

FOR 4–6

We love to cook with squid ink in the Basque country. For us, the ink is the essence of the squid – much more intense than the actual body. The mess one little bag of ink can make is incredible . . . This is the kind of food I love: rich and full of flavour. You need bread with this, big time.

300g dried chickpeas, soaked overnight (see method)

2 bay leaves

1 onion (for the chickpeas), peeled and cut in half

500g squid or cuttlefish (ask your fishmonger to clean them and to keep the skin and ink)

75ml extra virgin olive oil

3 cloves of garlic, finely sliced

2 onions, finely diced

1 red pepper, finely diced

1 green pepper, finely diced – or 16 Padrón peppers

150ml Txakoli (sparkling Basque wine), or sherry, or a crisp white wine

1 litre prawn stock (see page 288)

sea salt and freshly ground black pepper

Put the chickpeas into a large bowl (remember that they will double in size) and cover with plenty of hot water and an equal amount of sparkling water (this helps them to hydrate more quickly). The volume of water should be about four times the volume of the chickpeas. Leave to soak overnight.

The next day, drain the chickpeas and put them into a pan with plenty of fresh cold water, the bay leaf and onion. Place on a medium heat and bring to the boil, then lower the heat and cook until soft – around 40 minutes.

Cut the squid into rings, around one finger thick. Put the olive oil into a pan on a medium heat. When hot, fry the squid for a couple of minutes, then remove to a plate.

Add the garlic and diced onions to the same pan – you want to caramelize them for about 20 minutes (turn the heat down a little if they start to colour too quickly). Turn the heat down to low and add the peppers – again, you want to cook them slowly until they collapse into a mushy paste. The slower and longer you cook everything for, the more flavourful it will be.

Pour in the wine and stock, and add the cooked squid, its skin and ink. Then add the cooked chickpeas and season with salt and pepper. Continue to cook very gently until the sauce is thick.

Serve in bowls, with bread for dipping.

SQUID IN ITS OWN INK

I remember my mum cooking this when I was growing up . . . she used to prepare the squid herself and the ink would go everywhere! If you ask your fishmonger to clean and separate everything out for you it's a lot less messy.

Each mouthful of this dish tastes of the sea: it's rich, but delicate and smooth. When you get it right, it's heaven.

1kg squid, no larger than 100g in size (ask your fishmonger to clean them but to keep the wings, tentacles, skin and ink), or 12 baby squid

30ml olive oil

For the stuffing

50ml extra virgin olive oil

the squid trimmings (wings, tentacles and skin), finely diced

3 onions, finely diced

sea salt and freshly ground black pepper

For the ink sauce

60ml extra virgin olive oil

4 onions, finely diced

½ a large red pepper, finely diced

10 Padrón peppers

1 bay leaf

125g tomato sauce (see page 236)

50ml Txakoli (sparkling Basque wine), or sherry, or a crisp white wine

the squid ink (see above)

1 litre prawn stock (see page 288)

1 tablespoon (see page 283), to finish

To make the stuffing, put most of the olive oil into a pan on a medium heat and add the finely diced squid trimmings. They will release a lot of water – cook until this evaporates. Add the onions with a drizzle more olive oil and a pinch of salt, and allow to caramelize until soft and golden brown. The onions will shrink down a lot – you want to end up with the same quantity of cooked onion as squid. Season with salt and pepper.

To make the ink sauce, put the 60ml of olive oil into a casserole pan on a medium-low heat. Add the onions with a pinch of salt and cook until halfway caramelized, then add the peppers and bay leaf. When everything is very soft and almost paste-like, add the tomato sauce and wine. Cook until the alcohol evaporates, then add the squid ink and stock. Cook for 20 minutes, then whiz in a blender and put back on a medium-low heat.

Fill the squid bodies with the stuffing, using a small spoon, and close each one with a toothpick. The squid bodies should be about two-thirds full, to allow for expansion when they cook.

Put 30ml of olive oil into a pan on a medium heat, then add the stuffed squid and allow to caramelize on both sides. Add the stuffed squid to the ink sauce and cook on a low heat very gently for 30–40 minutes, until the squid is soft enough to cut through with a spoon. If the sauce looks like it is reducing too much, just add a little water.

Serve the squid and sauce in a bowl, with *ajillo* drizzled over and bread on the side for mopping up.

FISH & SHELLFISH

BOILED OCTOPUS WITH SMOKED SWEET PAPRIKA & 'CACHELOS' POTATOES

FOR 4–6

The amount of olive oil used in this recipe might seem like a lot, but the octopus needs it. Legend has it that drinking water with this dish will give you a pain in your stomach. What you need here is a nice glass of white wine, and Albariño, a traditional Galician white, is the best.

'Cachelos' refers to the potatoes, which are boiled in the octopus cooking water: crucially, they shouldn't be cut smoothly, you want to partially cut into them and then pull them apart so they make a scrunching sound. This way they will have a rough edge and release their starch.

½ an onion, peeled

1 bay leaf

1 frozen octopus (approx. 2.3kg before defrosting), defrosted

200ml extra virgin olive oil

1 tablespoon smoked sweet paprika, for sprinkling

50g capers

1 bunch of fresh chives, chopped

sea salt and freshly ground black pepper

For the potatoes

3 medium potatoes

125ml extra virgin olive oil

sea salt and freshly ground black pepper

1 tablespoon smoked hot paprika, for sprinkling

Fill a large pan with water, add the onion and bay leaf, and put on a medium-high heat. When the water is steaming, take the octopus and (carefully) dip it into the water, then bring it up again. Repeat three times. This relaxes the octopus, making the meat tender.

Gently simmer the octopus according to its weight (20 minutes per kilo) – if the water is boiling too fast it will rip the skin.

While the octopus is cooking, prepare the cachelos. Peel the potatoes. Partially cut into them, then pull them apart into chunky, uneven-edged pieces around 3cm in size.

To check if the octopus is cooked, take a toothpick and jab it into the thickest part. If it goes through cleanly, with no resistance, it is cooked, but if it feels like there's something preventing you from pushing through, then it needs to cook for longer, otherwise it will be chewy, which isn't nice. When you are happy it is cooked, carefully remove it from the pan to a tray (keeping the cooking water) and leave to cool down.

While the octopus is cooling, add the potatoes to the octopus cooking water and boil until nice and soft. The water will turn the potatoes a light blue-purple and will give them lots of flavour. Remove the potatoes to a colander with a spider or slotted spoon – don't pour them out to drain, as they will smash. Put into a serving bowl with the olive oil, salt, pepper and paprika. It's a lot of paprika, but you don't get tired of it.

Cut the octopus into 2cm thick angled chunks – it's traditional to use scissors, but probably easier to do this on a board with a knife! Put the 200ml of olive oil into a pan and put on a medium-low heat. When warm, add the chunks of octopus and cook for a couple of minutes. Take the pan off the heat but leave the octopus to rest for 3–4 minutes, then remove with a slotted spoon to your plate or serving dish. Dress with the olive oil from the pan, the paprika, capers, chives, salt and pepper, and serve with the potatoes.

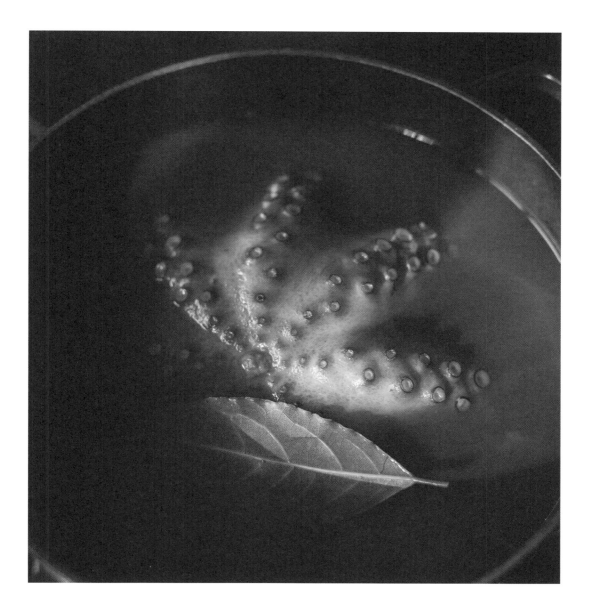

CHICKPEAS, PRAWNS & SQUID IN ADOBO FOR 4

Adobo is a thick, strong marinade made with a lot of spices: typically, these tend to include cumin, smoked paprika, oregano, garlic and bay leaf (and, when used with fish, vinegar). It's best to marinate overnight, or, if time is short, for a couple of hours at least. Cumin might not seem very Spanish but actually it is used a lot in the south of the country, due to the influence of Moorish food.

This is very quick: bar the overnight chickpea soaking and squid marinating, the actual cooking takes less than 10 minutes, as the *adobo* marinade helps to thicken the sauce so you don't need to spend time reducing it. The consistency shouldn't be too sauce-y but should be a little like chana masala. You could use tinned chickpeas, but the texture will be slightly different.

This is a rich dish, so you don't want a lot of it – it's great as a starter or as a smaller meal with a salad.

200g dried chickpeas, soaked overnight (see method)

1 bay leaf

1 onion, halved

300g squid, including tentacles (ask your fishmonger to clean them for you)

12 raw prawns, peeled and deveined

3 shallots, chopped

500ml prawn stock (see page 288)

sea salt and freshly ground black pepper

4 tablespoons chopped fresh flat-leaf parsley leaves

For the *adobo* marinade

150ml extra virgin olive oil

3 cloves of garlic, crushed

2 bay leaves

1 teaspoon ground cumin

1 teaspoon dried oregano

1 teaspoon smoked paprika

½ teaspoon hot paprika

Put the chickpeas into a large bowl (remember that they will double in size) and cover with plenty of hot water and an equal amount of sparkling water (this helps them to hydrate more quickly). The volume of water should be about four times the volume of the chickpeas.

The next day, drain the chickpeas and put them into a pan with fresh cold water, the bay leaf and the onion. Put on a medium heat and bring to the boil, then lower the heat and cook until they are nice and soft. Drain and set aside.

Cut the squid into rings, one finger thick. Put all the marinade ingredients into a bowl, add the squid and prawns and leave to marinate for a couple of hours.

Put a pan on a medium heat. When hot, add the marinated squid and let it caramelize for around a minute, then reduce the heat to low, add the prawns and fry for 30 seconds. Add the shallots and cook for a couple of minutes, until nice and soft, then add the drained chickpeas, stock, salt and pepper. Cook until slightly reduced and sauce-y, then stir together and serve, sprinkled with the parsley.

CUTTLEFISH & SAMFAINA

Samfaina is a Catalan vegetable dish made from courgettes, aubergines, red pepper and tomato, similar to ratatouille, though everything is chopped more finely. It is usually served as a sauce, typically alongside cod, though I love it with cuttlefish. Serve it in a terracotta dish with a big spoon for scooping up all the juices, and with plain rice to make it a main meal.

90ml extra virgin olive oil, plus more for finishing

1 large courgette, diced

sea salt and freshly ground black pepper

1 aubergine, diced

1 large red Spanish or Italian pepper, diced

2 cloves of garlic, thinly sliced

1 onion, diced

1 dried chilli

4 ripe tomatoes, diced

2 bay leaves

1 tablespoon smoked sweet paprika

125ml white wine

600g cleaned cuttlefish (allow 150g per person)

3 tablespoons chopped fresh flat-leaf parsley leaves

Put 15ml of olive oil into a pan on a medium heat. When hot, add the courgettes and season – you want them to colour and caramelize but retain their texture. When they reach this stage (around a couple of minutes), remove to a plate. Do the same with the aubergine, adding another 15ml of oil, and the same again with the red pepper, removing them all to the plate of courgettes.

Add another 15ml of olive oil to the same pan along with the garlic and onion – season and cook until soft and golden. Add the chilli, tomatoes and bay leaves and cook down to a paste. Then add the paprika and put all the caramelized vegetables back into the pan. Pour in the wine and season, then cook until the wine has evaporated – if it looks a little dry, add a splash of water.

Score the cuttlefish in diamonds.

Put the remaining 30ml of olive oil into another pan and put on a medium-high heat. When hot, add the cuttlefish – it will take around a minute and a half to caramelize each side (it will curl up). Season well and put on top of the *samfaina*, then sprinkle over the parsley and finish with a little more olive oil.

GALICIAN CRAB or CUTTLEFISH EMPANADA
MAKES 1 EMPANADA (FOR 6)

Traditionally *empanadas* are rectangular in shape. You can use pretty much anything in the filling: tuna is the classic, but cuttlefish is my favourite. One minute it's pale, and the next everything turns the deepest black . . .There is no specific time to eat an *empanada* – though any leftovers make a good breakfast.

500g good ready-made puff pastry

1 egg, whisked with a splash (15ml) of water, for brushing

sea salt and freshly ground black pepper

For the crab version

250g fresh or ready-prepared crabmeat (to cook your own, see method)

40ml extra virgin olive oil

4 shallots, finely diced

2 leeks, white part only, finely diced

1 bay leaf

150ml brandy

125ml white wine

500g tomato sauce (see page 236)

½ teaspoon cayenne pepper

250ml crab stock or prawn stock (see page 288)

For the cuttlefish version

90ml extra virgin olive oil

3 red onions, diced

2 bay leaves

14 Padrón peppers, diced

2 red peppers, diced

500g cuttlefish (ask your fishmonger to clean them and to keep the skin, ink and guts), cut into big cubes

100ml brandy

150ml white wine

1 litre crab stock or prawn stock (see page 288)

To make the crab filling

If you are cooking your crab, put it into a pan of cold salted water (so that the crab cooks more gently) and bring to the boil. I normally work to 12 minutes per pound (450g) of crab weight. A crab around 500g will need boiling for 14–15 minutes. Remove from the water and leave to cool before picking the meat.

Put the olive oil into a large pan on a medium heat. When hot, add the shallots and leeks and cook until they are really soft but without any colour. Add the bay leaf, brandy and wine. Cook until the alcohol has evaporated, then add the crabmeat, tomato sauce, cayenne pepper and stock. Season, then cook on a very gentle heat for 10–15 minutes, until it is thick enough not to run off a spoon. Leave to cool.

To make the cuttlefish filling

Put 50ml of olive oil into a large pan on a medium heat. When hot, add the onions and bay leaves and let them caramelize, then add the peppers. Cook until everything is nice and soft.

Put the remaining 40ml of olive oil into a separate pan on a medium-high heat and fry the cuttlefish quickly, so that it gets a little bit of colour.

Add the cuttlefish to the onions and peppers and mix together, then add the cuttlefish skin, ink and guts. Break up with a spoon, making sure the ink comes out. Add the brandy and wine and cook to evaporate the alcohol, then pour in the stock. Cook uncovered for an hour and a half, until the cuttlefish is meltingly tender – like butter. When everything is very thick and reduced, season with salt and pepper and leave to cool.

To make the *empanada*

Preheat the oven to 170–180°C, and lightly grease a 30cm x 20cm baking tray with olive oil.

Roll out 2 pieces of puff pastry until they are about 2mm thick and as large as your baking tray, with 3cm overhang. Transfer one piece of pastry to the tray and prick all over with a fork. Spread the cooled crab or cuttlefish mix over the pastry – the filling should not be too thick, not more than 1cm. Cover with the other piece of pastry. Seal the pastry by folding the edge over on itself, like a huge oblong raviolo, and make a hole in the middle of the *empanada* to let out the steam. Roll out any spare bits of pastry and use as decoration for the top of the *empanada.* Brush with the whisked egg and bake for 20 minutes.

Cut into squares. Eat warm or cold; it tastes even better the next day and should keep, refrigerated, for up to 3 days.

RAW PRAWNS & SCALLOPS WITH OLIVE OIL & LIME DRESSING

FOR 4

When you're using seafood of this quality, you don't want to overpower it. This is very light – the main flavour is the sweetness of the scallops. They shouldn't be sliced too thinly, as you want to be able to bite into them and use them to mop up the dressing. I use some Asian ingredients here, but that's all part of my flexible approach to recipes.

24 Cardigan Bay live prawns (or the very best-quality raw prawns you can find)

8 sustainable diver-caught live scallops (ask your fishmonger to clean them for you)

chopped fresh coriander leaves, to serve

micro red amaranth cress, or micro cress, or regular cress, to serve

For the dressing

100ml extra virgin olive oil

15ml sesame oil

25ml soy sauce

juice of 1 lime

sea salt and freshly ground black pepper

To make the dressing, mix all the ingredients together and whisk to emulsify.

Peel and devein the prawns. If they are small, leave them whole. If they are larger, cut them in half lengthways.

Cut each scallop horizontally into about 5 slices. Arrange the slices of scallop on plates with the prawns, drizzle over the dressing, and finish with the coriander and cress.

BAKED SCALLOPS WITH GARLIC & PARSLEY BREADCRUMBS

FOR 6

This is the kind of dish you find in a really old-fashioned, traditional restaurant where an elderly lady is cooking in the kitchen. It's quite a filling thing, as it's very rich: if you have one of these you won't want to eat much else. You could definitely have this as a main course with a salad, especially for lunch.

When cooking scallops, people often don't use the coral, but it has so much flavour, and in this recipe it turns the béchamel a lovely orange-red. It's great for making stocks with too.

8 large sustainable diver-caught scallops, fresh, on the shell

150g smoked pancetta

12 raw tiger prawns, peeled and deveined

75ml extra virgin olive oil

3 leeks, white part only, finely chopped

6 shallots, very finely chopped

240g unsalted butter

220g plain flour

1 litre whole milk

sea salt and freshly ground black pepper

1 bunch of fresh flat-leaf parsley, chopped

1 bunch of fresh chives, chopped

For the crumble

200g panko breadcrumbs

2 teaspoons cayenne pepper

1 teaspoon crushed garlic

3 tablespoons chopped fresh flat-leaf parsley leaves

sea salt and freshly ground black pepper

Use a flat, regular cutlery knife to open the scallops. They can be difficult to open, and you need to put a lot of strength behind it, so using a blunt knife is safer – or alternatively ask your fishmonger to open them for you.

Remove the muscle that attaches the scallop to its shell, keeping the meat and the coral. Chop both of these into small cubes.

Cut the pancetta and prawns to the same size as the scallops and corals.

Put the olive oil into a pan on a medium heat. When hot, add the chopped scallops. Fry briefly just to get a little colour, then remove from the pan. Cook the prawns in the same way, then remove. Add the pancetta, leeks and shallots to the pan and cook for a few minutes, until soft.

Add the butter to the pan and melt on a low-medium heat, then stir in the flour to make a paste. Add the milk slowly, stirring, until the mixture thickens to the consistency of béchamel. Season to taste – the pancetta will have made it quite salty already. Mix in the chopped scallops, corals and prawns and stir in the parsley and chives. Taste and make sure it is well seasoned. Leave to cool.

Spoon the mixture into six scallop shells to completely cover them, and smooth the surface with the back of a knife. Place them on a baking tray.

Preheat the oven to 200°C.

To make the crumble, mix together the panko, cayenne pepper, garlic, parsley, salt and pepper. Sprinkle the crumble on top of the filled scallop shells – you don't want it to be really thick, but you do want to cover the filling completely.

When the oven is hot, bake for 3–4 minutes or until the panko turns golden brown. Serve with little spoons.

MUSSELS A LA MARINERA

FOR 4–6

This is a really nice way to eat mussels. At Barrafina, we cook the mussels one by one so we can take them out of the pan the second they open, but that's not practical when cooking at home. One of the benefits of the method below is that all the mussel juice escapes into the tomato sauce. Serve with a glass of white wine and some bread – as is so often true, especially with Spanish food, the best bit about this dish is the dipping.

600g mussels

a drizzle of extra virgin olive oil

4 teaspoons chopped fresh flat-leaf parsley leaves

For the marinera sauce

75ml extra virgin olive oil

4 cloves of garlic, finely sliced

2 onions, roughly chopped into big chunks

1 red pepper, roughly chopped to the same size as the onions

2 bay leaves

1 teaspoon smoked paprika

200ml sherry or white wine

5–6 fresh ripe plum tomatoes

sea salt and freshly ground black pepper

To clean the mussels, wash them in a bowl of ice-cold water, then scrape any barnacles off the shells and remove the beards. Throw away any mussels with broken shells. Test if any slightly open mussels are still alive by squeezing the shells together – if they stay open, discard them. Drain and put into a bowl covered with a wet tea towel – this keeps them closed and happy.

To make the sauce, put the olive oil into a large pan on a medium heat. Add the garlic and onions and cook until slightly caramelized, then add the red pepper and bay leaves and sweat for around 15 minutes. Add the smoked paprika and sherry, cook until the alcohol has evaporated, then add the tomatoes. Cook for 20–30 minutes, stirring together to help everything break down and ensure the tomatoes get nice and sweet.

Put a drizzle of olive oil into a saucepan or a shallow casserole and place on a medium heat. Add the mussels, then scrape in the sauce, season with salt and pepper, and immediately put the lid on. Lower the heat slightly, then shuffle the pan to help release the mussel juices into the tomato sauce – they will open in 3 or 4 minutes.

Once the mussels have all opened (throw away any that haven't), sprinkle over the chopped parsley and serve.

CLAMS & ARTICHOKES

Dried chillies are often used in Basque cooking (in the *marmitako* on page 198, for example, or the clams in *salsa verde* on page 173), but there's usually no more than one. We don't generally like spicy food, but we like to feel that there's something there, as in the case of this recipe, which certainly isn't hot, but is lifted by the addition of the chilli.

The clam is the spoon here: use the shells to scoop up all the delicious sauce.

800g clams

fine sea salt, to clean the clams (see method)

60ml extra virgin olive oil

4 cloves of garlic, finely sliced

6 tablespoons chopped fresh flat-leaf parsley leaves

200ml white wine

25g plain flour

1 dried *guindilla* chilli, broken in half

250ml fish stock

sea salt and freshly ground black pepper

For the confit artichokes

20 baby artichokes

juice of 2½ lemons

a handful of fresh flat-leaf parsley stalks

1½ litres olive oil

2 heads of garlic, cut in half widthways

1 small bunch of fresh thyme

4 bay leaves

Check with your fishmonger whether the clams have been cleaned. If you need to clean them yourself, put them into a bowl of cold water with a tablespoon of fine salt and leave them for 40 minutes, moving them around gently every 10 minutes. The salt water makes them expel any sand.

To prepare the artichokes, first remove the top two layers of the leaves, then cut off the top third of the artichoke. With a small knife or a peeler, peel the artichokes from the bottom of the stalk to the top: you don't want to be able to see any dark green, just the pale layer underneath.

Put the peeled artichokes into a large bowl of water with the lemon juice and parsley stalks: these will stop the peeled artichokes discolouring while you prepare the rest.

Heat the 1½ litres of olive oil in a large pan and add the garlic and herbs. Drain and dry the artichokes, then add to the oil and let them cook on a very low heat (confit them) for 20–30 minutes, or until tender. Remove the artichokes from the pan and leave to drain, then cut in half.

Put 30ml of olive oil into a pan on a medium heat, then add the artichoke halves and caramelize on all sides until light golden brown. Remove from the pan.

Add another 30ml of olive oil to the pan, along with the garlic, and, when it starts to soften and turn golden, add 4 tablespoons of parsley. Pour in the wine and cook to evaporate the alcohol. Stir in the flour to thicken the sauce, then add the clams and dried chilli and stir again. Add the fish stock and stir vigorously. As soon as the clams start to open, put the artichokes back into the pan.

Season with a little salt and pepper and the remaining parsley, and serve.

CLAMS IN *SALSA VERDE*

This recipe is a family favourite. We always eat it as a starter at Christmas, and when it's served the table goes silent. The only noise is the sound of people eating – it's very sauce-y, so you use the clam shells as little spoons to scoop up the liquid. We only start to talk again when everyone's finished!

1kg clams

fine sea salt, to clean the clams (see method)

100ml extra virgin olive oil

4 cloves of garlic, finely chopped

1 bunch of fresh flat-leaf parsley, leaves finely chopped

200ml white wine

1 dried Cayenne pepper, broken in half

40g plain flour

650ml fish stock

sea salt and freshly ground black pepper

Check with your fishmonger whether the clams have been cleaned. If you need to clean them yourself, put them into a bowl of cold water with a tablespoon of fine salt and leave them for 40 minutes, moving them around gently every 10 minutes. The salt water makes them expel any sand.

Put the olive oil into a high-sided pan and put on a medium heat. Add the garlic and cook for 1 minute, then add half the parsley and the wine. Cook until the wine evaporates, then add the Cayenne and the flour. Stir, then add the fish stock. Continue stirring and, when it starts to come together, add the drained clams. Put the lid on quickly, and shake the pan a little to encourage the clams to open – you want them to open quickly in order to keep as much juice as possible inside the clams. Season with salt and pepper, and finish with the remaining chopped parsley.

COCO BEANS & CLAMS

It's very common to make a bean, chickpea or lentil stew at least once a week in Spain. We love pulses, and everyone always has dried beans at home. That said, I like to buy fresh coco beans (a white bean from France that is a variety of haricot) when they are in season. I think they're one of the best things in the world. They cook in 20 minutes and are really creamy – the skin disappears in your mouth. It's nice to use pulses in a different way: this is much lighter and quicker than a typical meat and bean stew, but still warming and good for scooping up with a spoon.

1kg clams

1 tablespoon fine sea salt, to clean the clams (see method)

500g coco beans (prepared weight)

75ml extra virgin olive oil

5 cloves of garlic, diced

2 onions, diced

1 leek, white part only, chopped

1 green pepper, diced

1 red pepper, diced

1 bay leaf

2 dried chillies, finely chopped

200ml white wine

1½–2 litres prawn stock (see page 288)

sea salt and freshly ground black pepper

½ a bunch of fresh chervil, chopped

Check with your fishmonger whether the clams have been cleaned. If you need to clean them yourself, put them into a bowl of cold water with a tablespoon of fine salt and leave them for 40 minutes, moving them around gently every 10 minutes. The salt water makes them expel any sand.

Pod and wash the fresh coco beans.

Put the olive oil into a large saucepan on a medium-low heat. When hot, add the garlic and onions and cook for 10–12 minutes. Add the leek and cook for 5–6 minutes, then add the peppers, bay leaf and dried chillies. Cook for around 8–10 minutes, until really soft and sweet but not coloured, then add the wine. Cook until the wine has evaporated, then add the stock and the coco beans. Half cover with the lid and steam very gently until the beans are nice and soft.

When the beans are ready, season with salt and pepper and add the clams. Half cover with the lid again, and as soon as the clams start to open, add the chopped chervil and mix everything together, seasoning again.

Serve with lots of bread, for mopping up the sauce.

COCKLES WITH PARSLEY, CHILLI & SHERRY

FOR 4

I like white-shelled cockles, as I find that the dark ones tend to be very sandy (I don't mind the odd bit of sand – it reminds you what you're eating – but you don't want the beach in your mouth). The best cockles I've ever tried were from the Isle of Wight: they were so juicy and full of flavour. This is the quickest, tastiest thing: you don't need any stock, as the wine and the juice from the cockles make the sauce.

1kg cockles

1 tablespoon fine sea salt, to clean the cockles (see method)

60ml extra virgin olive oil

6 cloves of garlic, thinly sliced

4 shallots, finely diced

1 bay leaf

2 fresh red chillies, thinly sliced

150ml sherry

1 bunch of fresh flat-leaf parsley, leaves picked

sea salt and freshly ground black pepper

To clean the cockles, put them into a bowl of cold water with the salt and leave for a couple of hours. Move them around gently every 10 minutes, rinsing them and changing the water frequently. The salt water makes them expel any sand.

Put the olive oil and garlic into a pan on a medium heat, then add the shallots and bay leaf. Cook gently for a minute, then add the chillies, cleaned cockles and sherry. The sherry will hiss – immediately put the lid on and turn up the heat slightly. You'll start to hear the clams pop open. When they have all opened, add the parsley leaves, then taste and add pepper and maybe salt.

Spoon into bowls and serve with some nice bread, for mopping up the sauce.

GRILLED RAZOR CLAMS *AL AJILLO*

I love shellfish cooked like this over a hot flat tray or *plancha*. In Spain, we don't really eat shellfish cold, we generally expect it to be hot. I think it's ten times more delicious when it's grilled and eaten straight away. All you really need for cooking razor clams is a tray or a flat grill.

12 medium-sized razor clams

sea salt and freshly ground black pepper

extra virgin olive oil, enough to drizzle over the pan

juice of 2 lemons

2 teaspoons ajillo (see page 283)

First, give the razor clams a good wash in cold salted water, then leave them in the water for 15–20 minutes to expel any sand.

You don't want to cook too many clams at once – if they are squashed they won't have room to open. Place around 5 clams on a flat tray or griddle (you won't be able to fit many in a round pan) and put on a medium-high heat. Drizzle a little bit of olive oil on top and leave them to open. Making sure they stay nice and flat, turn them over and cook them for 1 minute.

Squeeze over the lemon juice, remove to a long tray, season with salt and pepper, and finish with the ajillo.

OYSTER CEVICHE

There are hundreds of different types of ceviche or marinated raw fish: this one is very light and doesn't overpower the oysters. I always try to use the best oysters – which these are will depend on the time of year, so ask your fishmonger.

A note on opening oysters: always cover your fingers (holding the oyster) with a tea towel and use a pointy but blunt knife. I open them from the back, as you can see what you're doing more clearly.

1 fresh orange *aji amarillo* (Peruvian chilli), deseeded and very finely chopped – or use a mixture of green and red chillies

2 tablespoons very finely chopped fresh coriander leaves

¼ of a red onion, chopped very finely

1 stick of celery, chopped very finely

1 fresh red chilli, deseeded and chopped very finely

5–6cm piece of cucumber, skin off and deseeded, chopped very finely

juice of 1 lime

juice of ½ a lemon

juice of ½ an orange

25ml extra virgin olive oil

15ml Moscatel vinegar

12 oysters

Put all the chopped ingredients into a bowl. Add the liquid ingredients and stir to make a dressing.

Open the oysters, drizzle over the dressing and eat.

TXANGURRO

Everyone in Spain talks about *txangurro* from the Basque country, and once you've eaten it, you can see why.

Traditionally *txangurro* uses brown and white meat, but the brown meat from the spider crab – which is mostly in the head and legs – is even sweeter than that from a normal crab. This is usually served as a starter. It takes a bit of time, but the result is magic.

May to July is a good time for spider crabs in the UK (see page 293). You could use large brown crabs in their place (as pictured in these pages).

2 spider crabs (around 600g) or 1 large regular crab

1 bay leaf

For the sauce

50ml extra virgin olive oil

3 leeks, white part only, finely chopped

3 shallots, finely chopped

1 bay leaf

1 whole dried Cayenne pepper

100ml brandy

100ml white wine

150g tomato sauce (see page 236)

sea salt and freshly ground black pepper

To cook the crab, put it into a pan of cold salted water (the crab cooks more gently this way), add the bay leaf, and bring to the boil. Allow 20 minutes per spider crab, a little longer for a large regular crab.

Pick all the meat from the crab, cracking its legs, and keep the shell. There is very good brown meat in spider crabs: mix it all in with the white meat. Wash the shell.

To make the sauce, put the olive oil into a large pan on a low heat. Add the leeks and shallots and cook slowly until soft but not coloured – around 6–8 minutes. Add the bay leaf and pepper and continue cooking for a couple of minutes. Add the crabmeat and mix everything together, then pour in the brandy and wine and cook until the alcohol has evaporated. Finally add the tomato sauce and season with salt and pepper.

Spoon the crab mixture into the shells, and eat with a spoon, out of the shell.

SALT COD WITH PUMPKIN PURÉE & BLACK OLIVE SALAD

FOR 6

We use a lot of salt cod in the Basque country – this autumnal salad isn't a traditional recipe, but I love the colourful combination of ingredients, and the contrast between the creaminess of the pumpkin purée and the sharpness of the salad.

900g salt cod, cut into 150g portions and desalinated for 24 hours (see page 109)

1 pumpkin (preferably Delica) or butternut squash

100ml extra virgin olive oil

sea salt and freshly ground black pepper

8 sprigs of fresh rosemary, leaves picked

50g unsalted butter

For the black olive salad

100g unpitted black Aragón olives

1 small red onion, cut into thin julienne

20ml Pedro Ximénez (PX) balsamic vinegar

40ml extra virgin olive oil

sea salt and freshly ground black pepper

12 baby or small fresh basil leaves

First desalinate the cod (see page 109).

Preheat the oven to 180°C.

Peel the pumpkin, remove the seeds and cut into roughly 2½cm chunks. Line a large baking tray with greaseproof paper, then add the pumpkin. Drizzle over a couple of tablespoons of olive oil and season with salt, pepper and rosemary. Cover with foil and roast for 20 minutes.

When the pumpkin is nice and soft, put it into a blender or food processor with the butter, 40ml of olive oil, salt and pepper and blend to make a smooth purée. Keep warm.

Pit the olives – it doesn't matter if they break up. Mix with the red onion, balsamic vinegar, olive oil and a little salt and pepper.

Put 25ml of olive oil into a pan and put on a medium heat. When hot, add the desalinated salt cod fillets, skin side down, as many as will fit into the pan, and cook for 2–3 minutes. You want to get the skin really crispy – it has so much flavour, especially when it's been salted. Turn and cook for another minute for thinner fillets or 2–3 minutes if thicker. To check whether the cod is cooked, squeeze the sides: if the fish feels almost rubbery, with resistance in the middle, then it's not done yet. You could also pierce them with a toothpick to check – it should slide through easily. Repeat until all the fillets are cooked, adding more oil if needed.

Spoon the warm pumpkin purée on to plates, place the fried cod on top, skin side up, and spoon the salad around.

ALIOLI COD & POTATO GRATIN
WITH **SULTANAS**

FOR 4

This is a really warm, rustic dish with a sweet and sour flavour, and something I remember from when I was very young. The potatoes cooked in the chicken stock make a special kind of sauce.

50g sultanas

70ml sherry vinegar

4 small/ medium potatoes, cut into 1cm slices

2 onions, julienned

3 cloves of garlic, crushed

2 bay leaves

a sprinkling of fresh thyme leaves

75ml extra virgin olive oil, plus a little for drizzling

sea salt and freshly ground black pepper

500ml chicken stock (or use a mixture of white wine and water)

pine nuts, toasted

720g–1kg cod, cut into 150–180g portions

alioli (see page 287)

½ a bunch of fresh chervil, roughly chopped

Soak the sultanas in the vinegar overnight – this not only plumps them but gives them a sweet and sour flavour.

Preheat the oven to 170–180°C.

Put the potatoes and onions into a high-sided baking tray or roasting dish. Mix in the garlic, bay leaves, thyme and olive oil, using your hands, and season. Add the stock or wine and water, then cover with foil and bake in the oven for around 20 minutes. When the potatoes are juicy and cooked, sprinkle over the sultanas and the toasted pine nuts.

Turn on your grill.

Put the cod on a baking tray, drizzle with olive oil, season with salt and pepper, then cover with *alioli* and put under the grill – it should take 4–5 minutes for a thinner portion of cod, 8–10 minutes if it is on the thicker side. Squeeze the sides of the fish, and if you can feel any rubberiness in the middle it isn't cooked yet (you could also pierce it with a toothpick: if it goes through easily, it's done; if there's any resistance, then it isn't).

Sprinkle the chervil on top of the potatoes and serve with the cod.

WHOLE BRILL WITH GARLIC SAUCE

FOR 4–6

When you buy really fresh fish, you get this gelatine on the skin that feels like a sticky residue. Don't wash it off! That's the flavour of the fish and shows that it's fresh. This method of cooking works well with all the gelatinous flat fish: lemon sole, Dover sole, turbot, plaice . . . All it needs to accompany it is salad and bread.

4 whole brill
(around 1kg)

150ml extra
virgin olive oil

sea salt and
freshly ground
black pepper

3 cloves
of garlic,
thinly sliced

40ml Moscatel
vinegar

juice of ½
a lemon

smoked
paprika,
a sprinkle

4 tablespoons
chopped fresh
flat-leaf parsley
leaves

Put the tray you are going to cook the fish on into the oven, then preheat the oven to 200°C. You want the tray to get hot, so leave it in there for 8 minutes. The reason for this is that you want to cook the brill at a high temperature to get a crispy skin but ensure that it still has juicy flesh.

Put 25ml of olive oil on to a chopping board and toss the fish in the oil, seasoning on both sides.

Take the hot tray out of the oven (remember, it is hot!), and place the fish on it with the dark skin on top. Return to the oven and cook for around 18–20 minutes.

While the fish is in the oven, pour the remaining 125ml of olive oil into a small saucepan and put on a medium heat. Add the garlic and cook until softened and pale gold. You don't want it to crisp at all. Pour in the vinegar and lemon juice and whisk together – be careful when adding to the pan, as it will hiss. Add the paprika and chopped parsley and stir together.

When the fish is cooked, open the oven and pour over the dressing. Cook for another minute or so, then serve.

CLUB RANERO SALT COD

FOR 4–6

Juego de ranas is a popular game in the north of Spain where you throw coins into the mouth of an iron frog. All the bars have it, and, in summer, everyone plays on the street. Club Ranero ('the frog club') used to be famous years ago and would hold a tournament.

This recipe comes from the traditional Basque dish *bacalao pil pil*. The classic method is to put the salt cod, skin side up, into a terracotta pan and pour in enough olive oil to just cover the fish, along with crushed garlic, a bay leaf and chilli. As it cooks over a medium-low heat, the gelatine from the cod and the olive oil emulsify like a mayonnaise. When you see how it starts to change, it's almost like magic.

The story is that the chef at Club Ranero was making *bacalao pil pil* but there were too many people and he was short of sauce – so he made a new version, with peppers.

500g salt cod, cut into 4 pieces and desalinated for 24 hours (see page 109)

50ml extra virgin olive oil, plus at least 400ml to confit the cod

4 cloves of garlic, thinly sliced

3 onions, diced

1 x 220g tin of *piquillo* peppers, drained

16 Padrón peppers, chopped

3 dried *choricero* peppers, soaked for a couple of hours, then blended to a paste

2 dried chillies, soaked for a couple of hours, then blended to a paste

2 bay leaves

First desalinate the cod (see page 109).

Put 50ml of olive oil into a pan on a medium-low heat. Add the garlic, onions, peppers, *choriceros*, chillies and the bay leaves, and cook until the mixture becomes sweet and paste-like.

Add the cod to the pan, skin side up, plus enough olive oil to cover it, and lower the heat. If it is too hot the oil becomes thin; if you see the oil start to change, turn off the heat and keep it moving – it's like a dance. Swish the pan around until the oil emulsifies, the colour changes and everything becomes sticky. Serve with bread, to scoop up the juices.

GRILLED SEAFOOD SKEWERS
FOR 4 (2 SKEWERS PER PERSON)

This admittedly isn't very Spanish, but Asian marinades are a great way of injecting a lot of flavour very quickly. You really can't mess this up – it's always going to taste nice, especially if you cook it over charcoal. The size you chop the fish and vegetables is important here, as you want them to cook through without the marinade burning.

For the skewers

200g monkfish, cut into 3cm cubes

½ an onion, cut in half, then cut into three crossways and then lengthways, so you have chunks

½ a red pepper, cut into a similar size to the onion

200g tuna, cut into 3cm cubes

1 courgette, cut in half lengthways, then into 2cm cubes

8 raw prawns, peeled and deveined

40ml extra virgin olive oil, for cooking the skewers

For the marinade

100ml mirin

100ml soy sauce

25ml sesame oil

juice of 2 limes

3–4cm ginger

½ a bunch of fresh coriander leaves, chopped

2 cloves of garlic, crushed

For the dressing

25ml extra virgin olive oil

10ml Moscatel vinegar

sea salt

To serve

2 bunches of rocket or watercress

4 slices of bread, toasted

1 fresh red chilli, chopped

Mix all the marinade ingredients together.

Thread your skewers: first monkfish, then one piece each of onion, pepper, tuna, courgette and finally prawn. Make up all the skewers, then place them in a long, deep dish and cover with the marinade. Leave for a couple of hours, twisting the skewers round occasionally so that everything gets covered.

Heat your barbecue or grill, or put a pan on to heat, and cook the skewers with a little olive oil, turning them to colour all sides.

Whisk together the olive oil, vinegar and salt to make a dressing, and dress the rocket or watercress with it.

Serve the skewers on top of a piece of toast to soak up all the juices, with the chilli scattered over and the salad on the side. The way to eat this is to take one bite from the skewer, then one bite of bread.

SKATE with **CHORIZO** *PIPERRADA*

The first time I ate skate was with butter and capers, which is a very traditional, French way of cooking it. I love skate's meaty texture but it's a mild-flavoured fish by itself. *Piperrada* is a Basque dish of sautéd peppers and onions (sometimes with tomatoes). I add chorizo to it here, and the combination of the fat from the sausage and the sweetness from the peppers provides the punch the fish needs. When you get this dish right, it's so tasty and juicy, and easy to eat too – there's no fiddling around, you just have to push the flesh away from the bone. Skate isn't something we eat a lot in Spain, but it's unique in that it can be eaten both hot and cold. If you use jarred *piquillo* peppers instead of fresh, you can have this ready in 10 minutes.

80ml extra virgin olive oil

1 onion, julienned

1 red pepper, julienned

1 green pepper, julienned

200g whole *chorizotos* (baby chorizo)

1 bay leaf

565ml/1 pint of cider (Asturian or Aspall Suffolk cider)

sea salt and freshly ground black pepper

1kg skate wings (3cm thick portions – ask your fishmonger to skin them for you)

3 teaspoons chopped fresh flat-leaf parsley leaves

Put 15ml of olive oil into a pan on a medium heat. When hot, add the onions and peppers and cook for 15 minutes. Add the *chorizotos* and fry until they caramelize and start to lose some of their juices. Add the bay leaf and cider, then cook until reduced slightly and amalgamated with the chorizo juice to make a sauce (around 5–6 minutes). Season to taste.

Put the rest of the olive oil into a large pan on a medium heat. Season the skate with salt and pepper. Depending on the size of your pan, you might need to cook the fish in two batches. Fry the thickest side first, for around 4–5 minutes, then flip and season the other side and cook for around 2–3 minutes. To check if the skate is cooked, pierce with a knife to see if the flesh comes away from the bone. If it's still attached, give it another 30 seconds or so. Remove from the pan and leave to rest for a couple of minutes.

Serve the skate with the *chorizotos* and peppers on the side, and sprinkle over the chopped parsley.

GRILLED BREAM

I generally prefer to cook fish whole, as it has so much flavour and is more fun to eat. This is really simple: the most important thing is getting the skin right (don't even think about not eating the skin!). You want it to cook quickly, so it crisps and is juicy inside – if it cooks too slowly the skin won't become crispy.

It's expensive but, if you can afford it, look for wild bream: the scales should have a black dot parallel to the eye. You can use regular sea bream too.

100ml extra virgin olive oil

8 cloves of garlic

4 whole bream (around 600g – ask your fishmonger to scale and gut them for you)

4 bay leaves

½ a bunch of fresh thyme

1 lemon, cut in quarters

sea salt and freshly ground black pepper

4 tablespoons chilli oil

4 tablespoons *ajillo* (see page 283)

Preheat the oven to 200–220°C and put a baking tray, lightly greased with olive oil, in to warm up (alternatively, you can keep your fish in the pan if the handle is oven safe).

Smash the garlic and stuff it inside the bream with the herbs and lemon, squeezing the lemon a little. Massage the fish with plenty of olive oil, and season with salt and pepper.

Put the rest of the olive oil into a pan on a medium-high heat. Add the fish and cook for 1 minute on each side, just to get the skin crispy.

Transfer the fish to the tray and roast in the oven for 12–15 minutes.

Remove and finish with the chilli oil and *ajillo*. This is lovely with a green salad or something else green like samphire on the side.

MARMITAKO

This is one of the most typical of Basque dishes. If you don't have bonito, you can use tuna, which is very similar, or mackerel – an oily fish is basically what you're looking for.

A *marmita* is a big pot. It's what the fishermen use to cook with when they're out at sea and need something hot to keep them going – everything gets put in the one pot with the freshly caught fish.

175ml extra virgin olive oil

2 cloves of garlic, crushed

1 onion, finely diced

1 large red pepper, finely diced

200g Padrón peppers, finely diced

sea salt and freshly ground black pepper

1 bay leaf

2 dried *choricero* peppers, soaked in water overnight and flesh scooped out

1 fresh red chilli, deseeded and finely chopped

3 or 4 fresh ripe plum tomatoes, grated

200ml Txakoli (sparkling Basque wine), or sherry, or a crisp white wine

2–3 medium potatoes, peeled and cut into rough chunks

2 litres fish stock

2kg bonito (or 1kg fresh tuna)

1 bunch of fresh flat-leaf parsley, roughly chopped

Put 100ml of olive oil into a large pan on a medium-low heat. Add the garlic for 30 seconds, then add the onions and peppers and a pinch of salt and cook gently for 12–15 minutes.

Add the bay leaf, *choriceros*, chilli and grated tomatoes, and cook until paste-like. Pour in the wine and cook until the alcohol has evaporated. Add the potatoes and stir together with the paste so they're coated. Add the fish stock – the potatoes should be more or less covered. Cook for 15–20 minutes on a medium-low heat, until the potatoes are really nice and soft but not broken.

When the potatoes are cooked, cut the bonito into chunks the size of a 50p piece and season with a little salt and pepper. Put the remaining 75ml of olive oil into another pan on a medium-high heat and sear the bonito very quickly – you don't want to cook it through, just seal it so that it doesn't break up.

Add the bonito to the stew, take off the heat and mix everything together. Put the lid on the pan and leave for 5 minutes. Sprinkle over the chopped parsley and serve with bread, to scoop up the juices.

FISH & SHELLFISH

FISH & SHELLFISH

RICE with RED MULLET

When you go to Spain and have traditional paella or rice it might not seem like you're being given a lot of seafood, but what you can't see is how much has already gone into making the rice, via the stock. When your stock is good, your rice is good, as here.

80ml extra virgin olive oil

1 onion, julienned

1 bay leaf

150g very ripe tomatoes, cut in half

240g Bomba or Calasparra rice (60g per person)

800ml fish stock (see method)

½ a bunch of fresh basil

4 red mullet (filleted into 200g portions, or ask your fishmonger to fillet and pin-bone it for you, and to give you the bones)

For the stock

red mullet bones, roasted (see method)

20ml extra virgin olive oil, plus more for drizzling

sea salt and freshly ground black pepper

2 cloves of garlic, crushed

1 onion, diced

2 dried *choricero* peppers, soaked and cut in 3

1 dried red chilli, soaked and cut in 3

1 teaspoon smoked paprika

1½ litres prawn stock (see page 288)

Preheat your oven to 180°C. To make the stock, line a tray with baking paper and add the red mullet bones. Drizzle over a little olive oil and season with salt and pepper. Roast for 10–12 minutes, until golden brown.

Put the 20ml of the olive oil into a high-sided pan on a medium heat. Add the garlic and onion, season, and allow to caramelize for around 12 minutes. Add the *choriceros*, chilli and smoked paprika, and cook until it resembles a strong paste. Add the prawn stock and the roasted bones and cook on a very low heat, for 15–20 minutes. Place a sieve over a bowl, and strain so you are left with a smooth stock. You will need 800ml for this recipe.

To cook the rice, put 50ml of olive oil into a casserole pan on a medium heat. When hot, add the julienned onion and bay leaf and cook very slowly until golden brown (around 8–10 minutes). Add the tomatoes, using a fork to squeeze the juice out. Cook for 10 minutes, to bring everything together. Add the rice and cook for a couple of minutes to release the starch. Only then start to add the stock: just enough to cover the rice at first, then little by little, stirring continuously (almost as though you're making risotto) until the rice is al dente. Rip the basil – I always rip it, as cutting turns it black – and stir through the rice. Turn off the heat.

In the meantime, put the remaining 30ml of olive oil into another pan on a medium heat. When hot, add the red mullet, skin side down. Cook for 1½ minutes on the skin side to get it crisp, then season, turn and cook for 20–30 seconds on the other side. Serve the rice on plates with the mullet on top of the rice, skin side up. Drizzle with a little more olive oil, sprinkle with salt, and serve.

SEA TROUT, AUTUMN ROOT PURÉE & *MORCILLA*
FOR 4

Pan-fried sea trout with *jamón* (*trucha*) is a very typical dish of Navarra in northern Spain. This recipe is different, but it still combines surf and turf: it might sound cheffy but it's really just a case of using three ingredients: sea trout, which should have very crispy skin and be juicy and pink in the middle, sweet chervil or another wintery root, and spiced rice *morcilla*.

You will need to go to a really good market to find chervil root, which is in season from autumn to winter. If you can't get hold of it (and it is rare), you could make the purée with celeriac or parsnips, even potatoes – but if you do see chervil root when you're shopping, you should try it.

500g chervil root, celeriac or parsnips

600ml double cream

125ml extra virgin olive oil

25g unsalted butter

sea salt and freshly ground black pepper

150g rice *morcilla* (Spanish black pudding)

1 x 1kg or 2 x 500g sea trout (ask your fishmonger to fillet and pin-bone the fish for you)

½ a bunch of fresh chervil, leaves picked, roughly chopped

Fill a pan with water and heat until boiling. Add the chervil root (or other root vegetable) and cook until very soft – this won't take long. When it starts to float, it's done. Drain and peel while it is still hot (this way the skin comes off more easily). Put the peeled roots into a pan with the double cream, 50ml of olive oil, the butter, salt and pepper. Cook for a few minutes to bring together, then blend until very smooth. Put the lid on and keep warm.

Cut the *morcilla* into 2cm thick medallions. Put a frying pan on a low heat and fry the *morcilla* until caramelized on the outside but still moist inside – it burns very quickly, so this will only take 30 seconds or so.

Rinse out your frying pan, add the remaining 75ml of olive oil and put on a medium heat. When hot, place the sea trout in the pan, skin side down, and cook for 2 minutes, until crispy. If you want to check it's cooked, don't turn it over but lift it slightly at the side to have a peek. When you're happy it's ready, turn and cook the other side very quickly, just for 5 seconds or so, then remove from the pan.

Spoon the root purée on to a plate. Place the black pudding on top, then the sea trout, skin side up. Sprinkle salt over the crispy fish skin and finish with the chopped chervil leaves.

FISH & SHELLFISH

SEAFOOD STEW

This stew, *caldereta de pescado*, is a real feast, the type of recipe that's perfect for a special occasion. There are a lot of ingredients, but everything goes into the same pot for maximum flavour.

Picada means 'very finely chopped'. Generally in Spanish cooking the *picada* is added at the end, to give a dish (often a stew like this) a final punch of flavour and some extra texture. Despite its meaning, it's often made in a pestle and mortar, as here.

For the stock

50ml extra virgin olive oil

2 leeks, white and green parts, diced

3 carrots, peeled and diced

1 onion, peeled and diced

6 sticks of celery, diced

6 cloves of garlic, smashed

3 fresh bay leaves

1½ tablespoons tomato purée

2 dried *choricero* peppers, soaked and chopped

1 dried *ñora* pepper, soaked and chopped

20–24 shell-on raw prawns (ask your fishmonger for a mixture of prawns for maximum flavour)

2 teaspoons sweet paprika

125ml dry white wine

80ml Ricard

125ml Spanish brandy

125ml Fino or Manzanilla sherry

To make the stock, heat the oil in a large saucepan. Add the leeks, carrots, onion, celery, garlic and bay leaves. Stir in the tomato purée, and the *choricero* and *ñora* peppers. Cook over a low-medium heat for 45 minutes, stirring frequently, until the vegetables are thoroughly caramelized. Add the prawns and the paprika, stir, then add the wine, Ricard, brandy and sherry. Turn the heat up to evaporate the alcohol, then add just enough water to cover the vegetables and simmer gently for a further 45 minutes. Remove from the heat.

Strain the stock through a sieve over a large bowl, squeezing down on the prawns and vegetables.

To make the *picada*, put the garlic and parsley into a pestle and mortar and bash together, then add the nuts and keep bashing until everything is in little pieces. Add a little olive oil to loosen if necessary.

To make the stew, heat 50ml of olive oil in a large pan on a medium heat, then add the onions and cook gently for 5 minutes, until soft but not coloured. Add the saffron and stir for a minute. Add the tomatoes and cook for a further 5 minutes, then add the potatoes. Add the stock and simmer for 7 minutes, until the potatoes are cooked, then turn the heat down to medium-low.

For the stew

75ml extra virgin olive oil

1 onion, finely diced

4 or 5 strands of saffron

100g ripe tomatoes, peeled and chopped

300g potatoes, peeled and diced

4 medium squid, cleaned and chopped into rings

1 large live brown crab (ask your fishmonger to cut this into large chunks for you – make sure you use it on the day you buy it)

4 langoustines, sliced in half lengthways

400g fish fillets, cut into 50g chunks (monkfish, red mullet, hake and gurnard)

6 mussels

4 razor clams

sea salt and freshly ground black pepper

2 slices of good white bread

1 clove of garlic, peeled and sliced

For the picada

2 cloves of garlic, peeled

a small bunch of fresh flat-leaf parsley

50g whole blanched hazelnuts, lightly toasted

50g whole blanched almonds, lightly toasted

Put the remaining oil into a flat pan on a medium-high heat. Season the squid and fry quickly so that it colours slightly, then add to the pan with the stock. Do the same with the crab pieces, the langoustines and finally the fish. Turn the heat down to low, then add the mussels and clams to the stew and half cover.

When the stew is very gently bubbling, stir in the *picada* and leave for a couple of minutes. Taste and adjust the seasoning if necessary, then turn off the heat.

Toast the bread on both sides in a pan with a little olive oil until nice and crispy, then rub with the raw garlic clove.

Serve in bowls, with the toast for dipping.

My parents are from Extremadura, in south-west Spain, an area famous for its Iberian pigs and for producing the very best *jamón*. We used to go on holiday there when I was a child, and when we came back home to Santurtzi our car would be full of sausages that we'd made from a pig we'd slaughtered. At home, we had a *trastero* (storage room), not much more than a small dark hole with a door, and we'd hang all our homemade chorizo and *morcilla* inside there to cure. Every time you opened the door you would get a waft of cured meat. When I came back from school, before going on to judo or whatever sports I was doing, I'd cut off a small slice of *morcilla* or chorizo with a little knife and sandwich it in between pieces of bread for a snack. Now, when I go to the market in Bilbao the smell of the chorizo and *morcilla* reminds me of the *trastero* at home.

Santurtzi is a port town, so fish is pretty abundant, but growing up we'd eat meat a couple of times a week, probably, whether it was my mum's braised rabbit (see page 222) or the one-pan chicken in garlic sauce (see page 213). And, of course, there was always the *trastero* to raid. My mum would always try to ensure that no part of the animals she cooked was wasted, so we ate a lot of offal too. It's probably not surprising that, for me, these less popular cuts of meat still taste the best (the pan-fried sweetbreads on page 252 are a favourite). They are cheap, but you do need to pay attention to them: on the one hand, it's important not to overcook livers and kidneys or they'll be tough, but on the other, cuts like pig's cheeks and ears need slow braising to get to the tender, melt-in-the-mouth stage where they fall off the bone. The main thing I learned from my mother's cooking, and I apply it to my menus now, is that you don't need to buy premium cuts to enjoy the best meat.

MY FIRST CHICKEN

I think I was nine when I cooked my first chicken. We had a small oven, like a microwave, so it was very easy for me to look inside and see when the chicken was crispy and juicy. In Spain, there are a lot of places (*pollerías*) that sell good-quality whole roast chickens to take away – they're very popular, and you often see families queueing up to get their chicken. Sometimes my parents would pick one up on a Sunday, on their way back from dancing, when it was too late to cook. When I cooked my chicken, I added beer and white wine and lemon. You don't taste the alcohol: the beer, wine and lemon combine with the juices of the chicken to make a delicious sauce. You can eat a whole loaf of bread by dipping it into this sauce. After I made it, I remember my father saying, 'How can she make chicken so good?' Three or four weeks later I tried again and it went wrong. I don't know why. But I was very disappointed. It's a good lesson to realize that it's not always easy to get it right . . .

Serve with salad, *patatas a lo pobre* (see page 214) and lots of bread.

1 free-range chicken, around 1.2kg

20ml extra virgin olive oil

sea salt and freshly ground black pepper

1 whole head of garlic, divided into cloves

2 bay leaves

½ a bunch of fresh thyme

1 can (330ml) of lager

225ml white wine

juice of 1 lemon

Preheat your oven to 180–190°C.

To spatchcock your chicken, cut along either side of the backbone with sharp kitchen scissors. Open the chicken out and press down on it to flatten, then turn round and press down again. Rub the olive oil into the chicken skin and season.

Squash the cloves of garlic and place in the bottom of a high-sided roasting tray with the bay leaves and thyme. Put the chicken on top.

Roast for 25 minutes, then mix the beer, wine and lemon juice together and pour into the tray. Cook for another 20 minutes, continuing to baste the chicken every 5–7 minutes, leaving the skin to crisp for the last 10 minutes.

CHICKEN IN GARLIC SAUCE

FOR 4

Pollo al ajillo is something I'd often have as a kid. But it's not just for children: for me, this is the quickest and best way to cook chicken. The flavours are balanced: there is acidity and freshness from the lemon and parsley that are added at the last minute, and a slight kick from the chillies. It's versatile too: it makes perfect finger food, or you could add some salad and bread on the side to make it more of a main. The sauce that is created from the chicken juices and oil is made for dipping, so bread – as always – is important.

A wok isn't Spanish, obviously, but it's good for cooking this recipe, as you need to keep everything moving, and with a wok the oil stays in the pan. Even my mum has a little wok!

80ml extra virgin olive oil

1 chicken, about 1–1.2kg, jointed, then cut into 50p size pieces (or 1–1.2kg thighs/legs/breasts) – skin on

sea salt and freshly ground black pepper

16 cloves of garlic, skin on, smashed with the back of a knife

2 fresh red chillies, sliced in half lengthways (keep the seeds)

2 bay leaves

zest and juice of 2 lemons

1 bunch of fresh flat-leaf parsley (approx. 50g), roughly chopped

Put the olive oil into a wok or a large frying pan on a medium heat. When smoking, add the chicken to the pan and season a little. Cook, tossing, until every part of the chicken gets really caramelized and golden brown (this should take around 12–15 minutes) and the skin is very crisp.

Halfway through this time – so, after about 6 minutes – add the smashed garlic. When the garlic starts to get a little golden, add the chillies and bay leaves. Cook for a minute, keeping everything moving in the pan, then add the lemon zest and juice, with the parsley.

Take off the heat, season to taste, and serve.

CHICKEN & MOJO ROJO
& PATATAS A LO POBRE

FOR 3–4

Mojo rojo comes from the Canary Islands and is the kind of sauce that lifts the flavour of anything. It's good for children, as it's full of flavour without being too spicy – and big children like it too.

With the *patatas a lo pobre* ('poor man's potatoes') the only ingredients apart from the potatoes are olive oil, an onion and a bay leaf, so you need to be generous with the seasoning. They should be very soft, almost like confit potatoes.

1 free-range chicken, about 1.2kg, cut into portions (or 6–8 chicken thighs)

For the mojo rojo

1 tablespoon fennel seeds

8 cloves of garlic

2 tablespoons ground chilli

1 tablespoon cumin seeds

1 teaspoon smoked sweet paprika

20ml sherry vinegar

150ml extra virgin olive oil

sea salt and freshly ground black pepper

For the patatas a lo pobre

4 medium potatoes

1 onion, cut in thick julienne (around ½cm)

1 bay leaf

200ml extra virgin olive oil

400ml water

sea salt and freshly ground black pepper

Blend all the *mojo rojo* ingredients together, adding enough water to make a dribble-able, sauce-like consistency. Rub it into the chicken and leave it in the fridge overnight to marinate.

Preheat the oven to 170–180°C.

Put the chicken into a roasting tray lined with greaseproof paper, skin side up, and roast for 40–45 minutes, or around 20 minutes if just cooking thighs.

As soon as you've put the chicken into the oven, peel the potatoes and cut into 1cm slices. Line a second roasting tray or a baking tray with greaseproof paper (making sure there is plenty of paper overhanging – you will need to be able to get hold of it and lift it up later). Put the potatoes into the tray along with the onion, bay leaf, olive oil, water, and a generous amount of salt and pepper.

After the chicken has been in the oven for 20–25 minutes, put the tray of potatoes into the oven. Roast for 10–15 minutes, keeping an eye on them, and when you see the top of the potatoes becoming slightly coloured, lift up the paper and tip the potatoes out into the roasting tray, so the other side can cook for another 10 or so minutes, by which time the chicken should also be ready.

Serve the chicken and potatoes together, with a Little Gem salad.

RICE with CHICKEN & *PISTO*

Using bone-in chicken serves two purposes: it adds more flavour to the rice and it ensures the chicken stays juicy. Just remember the bones when you come to eat. *Pisto* is a vegetable stew, and adds an extra element of flavour to the rice here.

75ml extra virgin olive oil

4 large chicken thighs, skin on, bone in, quartered

sea salt and freshly ground black pepper

½ an aubergine, diced

½ a courgette, diced

½ a red pepper, diced

1 red onion, diced

720ml chicken stock

4 cloves of garlic, finely sliced

1 bay leaf

2 tablespoons tomato purée

100ml white wine

1 tablespoon sweet smoked paprika

360g Calasparra rice (or Bomba or any other good rice)

4 tablespoons finely chopped fresh chives

Put 45ml of olive oil into a large shallow casserole dish or sauté pan on a medium heat, then add the chicken, skin side down, season a little, and cook until the skin is crispy, around 2–3 minutes. Turn and cook for another minute, then remove the chicken from the pan to a large plate.

Add the aubergine to the pan, season a little, and cook until slightly coloured, soft and cooked through, around 6–7 minutes. Remove to the plate with the chicken.

Add a tablespoon more oil, then add the courgettes and season a little. When they start to caramelize (around 2 minutes), add the red pepper and cook for another couple of minutes. Next, add the red onion and cook until slightly coloured, around 3–4 minutes, stirring with a spoon. Remove all the vegetables to the plate with the aubergine and chicken.

Have your stock ready: you don't want it boiling or it will reduce (if it does, just top it up with water), but it should be steaming.

Add another tablespoon of oil to the pan and put in the garlic. Stir, and when it starts to turn golden, put everything from the plate back into the pan. Add the bay leaf and tomato purée, stir together to mix, then leave for a minute.

Pour in the wine and cook to evaporate, then add the paprika and rice. Stir together, then cook for a couple of minutes, continuing to stir with a spoon to remove the starch from the rice.

Lower the heat to a gentle medium-low and add a quarter of the stock to the pan, stirring with a spoon. When the stock evaporates, add more. Make sure the heat is medium-low, otherwise the stock will evaporate too fast without cooking the rice. Continue doing this, stirring frequently, until you have used all the stock. Taste the rice: if you prefer it less al dente, just add a splash more water and cook it for a bit longer – doing this won't dilute the flavour.

When you're happy with the rice's texture, season again if necessary, then serve, sprinkled with the chopped chives.

MARINATED GRILLED QUAIL with HONEY

FOR 4

If I'm eating fish or chicken I generally like to cook it with the bones in to keep it moist, but with quail there are so many small bones that you have to work really hard to eat any meat.

Ask your butcher nicely to clean and butterfly the quail for you; I guarantee that when you've cooked it this way, you'll find that you like it even more than chicken. Unlike chicken, quail should be cooked medium so it stays juicy.

For the quail

4 jumbo quail (prepared as above)

2 dried red chillies, soaked in warm water for a couple of hours

60ml extra virgin olive oil

sea salt and freshly ground black pepper

3 tablespoons chopped fresh coriander leaves

½ a bunch of peppery salad leaves (e.g. rocket or watercress)

15ml Moscatel vinegar

For the marinade

100ml pomace or light olive oil

2 cloves of garlic, crushed

2 bay leaves

½ a bunch of fresh lemon thyme

1 dried chilli

To infuse the honey

125ml orange blossom honey

2 cloves

3 star anise

1 dried chilli

1 teaspoon white peppercorns

Mix the marinade ingredients together, then massage into the quail and leave for at least 4 hours and ideally overnight.

Deseed the soaked chillies and chop into rings, then cover with half the olive oil and mix together. Leave to sit; the oil should turn red.

In a saucepan, on a really low heat, gently infuse the honey with the cloves, star anise, chilli and peppercorns. Do not leave the pan of honey while it is on the heat!

Put a pan on a medium heat. Season the quail and add to the pan, skin side down – make sure there's not too much excess oil, just enough to spread over the body of the quail. When the skin is golden and crispy (around 3–4 minutes), turn the quail over and cook for another 30–40 seconds, then season again.

Take the quail from the pan and put them on a tray or plate, skin side up, then drizzle over the chilli-infused oil and honey.

To serve, put a quail on one side of each plate and sprinkle over the coriander, then add the salad leaves (dressed at the last minute with the rest of the olive oil and the vinegar) on the other side.

MY MUM'S BRAISED RABBIT IN SALSA

FOR 4

This is one of my mum's specialities. Every time friends or family came to our house, they'd ask her to make this dish – and they'd always have seconds. It's so tasty that you can just keep eating and eating. Even though we've cooked it together, I don't know what she does – it's never the same when I make it. People often think that rabbit is dry but it really isn't. The meat should fall off the bones.

50ml extra virgin olive oil, plus a little extra

1 whole rabbit (ask your butcher to portion your rabbit for you – this is the cheapest way – or buy the shoulder only and cut it in half)

sea salt and freshly ground black pepper

1 onion, cut in thick julienne

4 cloves of garlic, finely sliced

1 leek, sliced on an angle

2 sticks of celery, sliced on an angle

2–3 carrots, sliced on an angle

4 ripe tomatoes, cut into cubes

2 dried *choricero* peppers, roughly chopped

2 dried red chillies, roughly chopped

2 bay leaves

200ml white wine

1 litre chicken stock

3 teaspoons chopped fresh flat-leaf parsley leaves

Put the olive oil into a pan on a medium heat and cook the pieces of rabbit until browned. Remove and season.

Add a little more oil to the pan, then add the onions and garlic. When the onions start to turn golden brown, add the leek and celery and let them caramelize, then add the carrots and cook until softened. At this point, add the tomatoes and cook down until the mixtures is paste-like to make a *sofrito* – you want to get rid of the tomatoes' acidity and cook off the water. Season to taste.

When the *sofrito* is slightly reduced and everything has come together, add the dried *choriceros* and chillies, the bay leaves, salt and pepper and cook for a minute, then add the wine. Cook to evaporate the alcohol (you're looking for it to cook down and no longer be liquid), then add the chicken stock. Put the rabbit back into the pan, cover with the lid and cook on a very gentle low-medium heat for around 40 minutes. It is ready when you can see the meat fall from the bone.

Finish with the chopped parsley and serve with *patatas a lo pobre* (see page 214).

PORK BELLY & MOJO VERDE

FOR 6–8

This recipe uses a pestle and mortar to make a lumpier *mojo verde* that's good for serving alongside meat, but you could make a smoother, creamier sauce for marinating. Just put all the ingredients, except the coriander, into a blender. Whiz together, adding the coriander halfway through, then blend again until green and creamy with some small flecks of herb.

Instead of pork belly, you could grill lamb cutlets and serve them with the *mojo verde* dotted around, or marinate chicken in the smoother version of the sauce.

1 x 4–5kg piece of pork belly, rib bones intact

sea salt and freshly ground black pepper

2 tablespoons cumin seeds

extra virgin olive oil, for drizzling

For the *mojo verde*

1 bunch of spring onions

4 cloves of garlic

2 big bunches of fresh coriander (equal to around 6–8 of the 40g supermarket packets)

2 teaspoons cumin seeds

125ml Moscatel vinegar

2 dried chillies

sea salt and freshly ground black pepper, to taste

200ml extra virgin olive oil

Preheat the oven to 180°C.

Line a roasting tray with greaseproof paper. Score the skin of the pork belly quite deeply (around 1cm), then place it skin side down on the paper-lined tray. Season the top of the pork belly with salt, pepper and cumin seeds and cook for 1½–2 hours. The skin should be very crispy and the meat must be tender – if it's not quite there yet, turn it over and cook it for another 10 minutes.

Make the *mojo verde* while the pork belly is cooking: roughly chop the spring onions, garlic and herbs and add them gradually to a pestle and mortar with the rest of the ingredients, dribbling in the olive oil bit by bit and mashing together.

Spoon some *mojo verde* on to each plate, then top with 1–2cm thick pork belly slices and drizzle over a little olive oil to finish.

BRAISED IBERIAN PORK RIBS

I always cut ribs into small sections, against the bone. This is common in Spain: it looks more elegant, and you can eat the ribs with a knife and fork, instead of with your hands.

These ribs are best started on a charcoal barbecue, as this gives them that smoky flavour. But you can also pan-fry them until golden brown, then braise them in the oven. Iberian pork ribs are really fatty, so when you braise them they become very glazed and sticky. If you use regular pork ribs, you will need to add slightly more liquid and reduce it further.

Mashed potato works well with this dish – the combination of creamy with sticky is a good one.

a little olive oil, if using a pan

2kg Iberian pork ribs (ask your butcher to cut them into 3 sections against the bone)

2 onions, cut in half

2 leeks, cleaned

4 sticks of celery

3 carrots, peeled

8 plum tomatoes

3 litres chicken stock

150ml orange blossom honey

150ml Pedro Ximénez (PX) balsamic vinegar

2 bay leaves

2 dried chillies

fronds from 2 fennel bulbs (save the bulbs for the tomato, fennel and avocado salad, page 99)

Preheat the oven to 160–170°C.

Heat your barbecue or pan (if the latter, add a little oil). Add the ribs and let them caramelize, then place in a roasting tray.

Add the onions to the barbecue or pan and char on both sides, then do the same with the whole leeks, celery, carrots and tomatoes.

Cut all the charred vegetables into quite thick chunks (around 2cm), on an angle. Add to the roasting tray with the chicken stock, honey, vinegar, bay leaves and chillies, then braise for 2½–3 hours.

When the meat is very tender, you want to make the cooking liquid and juices sticky. This may have happened already in the oven but, if it hasn't, pour the liquid off into a saucepan and cook until reduced.

Pour the sauce over the ribs and sprinkle over the fennel fronds.

PORK LOIN IN ADOBO & BÉCHAMEL SAUCE WITH BROKEN POTATOES

This is a good Saturday or Sunday meal – the sort of thing where you bring one dish to the middle of the table to serve up. The potatoes are perfect for mopping up the béchamel.

1kg pork loin (Iberian or good-quality white pork loin: ask your butcher to cut it into 8 x 1cm steaks)

60ml extra virgin olive oil

sea salt and freshly ground black pepper

125g Manchego cheese

For the adobo marinade

1 tablespoon ground cumin

1 tablespoon dried oregano

1 teaspoon smoked paprika

2 cloves of garlic, crushed

2 bay leaves

½ a bunch of thyme, leaves picked

175ml extra virgin olive oil

For the béchamel

2 litres whole milk

240g unsalted butter

220g plain flour

sea salt and freshly ground black pepper

a pinch of grated nutmeg

For the potatoes

1kg baby potatoes

sea salt and freshly ground black pepper

2 bay leaves

60ml extra virgin olive oil

1 teaspoon smoked paprika

3 tablespoons chopped fresh flat-leaf parsley

Make the adobo by mixing all the ingredients together to make a wet rub. Massage into the pork and leave in the fridge overnight to marinate.

Preheat the oven to 180°C. Boil the potatoes in salted water with the bay leaves until they are nice and tender – around 12–15 minutes.

While the potatoes are cooking, make the béchamel. Warm the milk in a pan on a low heat. In a separate pan, add the butter and melt on a low heat. Add the flour and mix together well, then cook for 1 minute. Start to add the warmed milk: add a quarter at first, mixing together all the time, then add another quarter and mix again. Continue cooking and mixing until you have used up all the milk (add it little by little now, as you want to keep the béchamel thick and creamy). You need to cook it for 20 minutes to cook off the flour. Season and add the grated nutmeg at the end.

Put 60ml of olive oil into a pan on a medium heat and caramelize the pork loin steaks, then remove to a baking tray and season. Cover with the béchamel and bake in the oven for 10–12 minutes. A couple of minutes before it's ready, sprinkle over the grated Manchego and cook until golden brown.

While the pork is in the oven, drain the potatoes and leave to cool slightly, then remove to a pan. Squash each potato by pushing down on it with a knife. Add 60ml of olive oil to the pan and cook on a medium heat for 2–3 minutes, until the potatoes are golden brown and crispy, moving them around occasionally. Season and sprinkle over the paprika and parsley.

Put the pork and potatoes into a dish and serve.

BUTIFARRA, CARAMELIZED ONIONS & SHERRY

FOR 4–6

Butifarra is a sausage from Catalonia. There are two types: fresh and boiled. This recipe uses the fresh sort, as it stays firm – boiled *butifarra* would fall apart, though it is delicious when you pan-fry it, as you get this caramelized sticky sugar on the sausage . . . All you need for eating fried boiled *butifarra* is a piece of bread – just sandwich it in.

60ml extra virgin olive oil, plus a little extra to finish

1kg *butifarra*

3 cloves of garlic, thinly sliced

3 onions, julienned

sea salt and freshly ground black pepper

½ a bunch of fresh thyme

2 bay leaves

250ml sherry

1 litre chicken stock or water

3 tablespoons chopped fresh flat-leaf parsley leaves

Preheat the oven to 180–200°C.

Put the olive oil into a large pan or a shallow casserole dish on a medium heat. Add the *butifarra* and let it caramelize, then take it out of the pan.

Add the garlic to the pan and when it starts to turn golden, add the onions with a pinch of salt and a grind of pepper. Cook until the onions are golden brown, then add the thyme and bay leaves. Pour in the sherry and cook until evaporated.

Cut the *butifarra* into 4 pieces and add to the pan, with just enough stock or water to cover the onions. Season and cook in the oven, uncovered, until the top of the *butifarra* turns slightly golden.

Finish with the chopped parsley and a drizzle of olive oil. Serve with good bread, to scoop up the juices.

PIG'S TROTTERS IN SPICY TOMATO SAUCE

FOR 4

This is one of my childhood favourites. It's real finger food: you use your knife and fork at first, but then you have to get into it and suck the bones. I like to add a bag of soaked dried chickpeas while cooking the trotters – this gives the stock a more rustic, intense flavour and you can use the cooked chickpeas to make a salad.

8 whole pig's trotters (ask your butcher to get them for you)

250g dried chickpeas, soaked overnight in water, tied up in muslin

2 bay leaves

1 leek, diced

2 carrots, roughly chopped

1 onion, roughly chopped

For the spicy tomato sauce

250ml extra virgin olive oil

2 onions, finely diced

3 carrots, finely diced

2 leeks, white part only, finely diced

1 bay leaf

150g pancetta, diced

150g chorizo, diced

2 dried *choricero* peppers, soaked in water and finely chopped

4 dried chillies, soaked in water and finely chopped

1 teaspoon smoked paprika

1kg good-quality tinned plum tomatoes, blitzed

sea salt and freshly ground black pepper

2 teaspoons sugar, or to taste

Preheat the oven to 170–180°C. Clean and wash the trotters thoroughly, and burn off any hair.

Fill a large deep ovenproof pan with water and bring to the boil. Blanch the trotters, then change the water and bring to the boil again. Add the trotters, the muslin bag of chickpeas, the bay leaves, leek, carrots and onion. Cover with a lid or foil and braise for 2 hours, until the meat is tender enough to fall off the bone but the trotters are still intact. Remove the trotters from the pan and discard the vegetables, but keep the chickpeas and cooking liquid. Pass the liquid through a sieve.

While the trotters are cooking, make the sauce: put the olive oil into a pan on a medium heat, then add the onions and cook until caramelized. Add the carrots, leeks and bay leaf and cook until all the vegetables are very soft and mushy (the longer you cook them the sweeter the sauce will be). Add the pancetta and chorizo and cook until they release their fat. Next add the sliced *choriceros*, dried chillies, smoked paprika and blitzed tomatoes, season with salt and pepper, and cook until the sauce begins bubbling: taste it and add sugar depending on how sweet the tomatoes are.

Season the trotters, then add to the tomato sauce with 1 litre of the sieved cooking liquid. Cook for another 30–40 minutes, until the flavours meld together: the gelatinousness of the trotters will make the sauce thick and sticky.

Serve one trotter, per person, with bread to scoop up the juices.

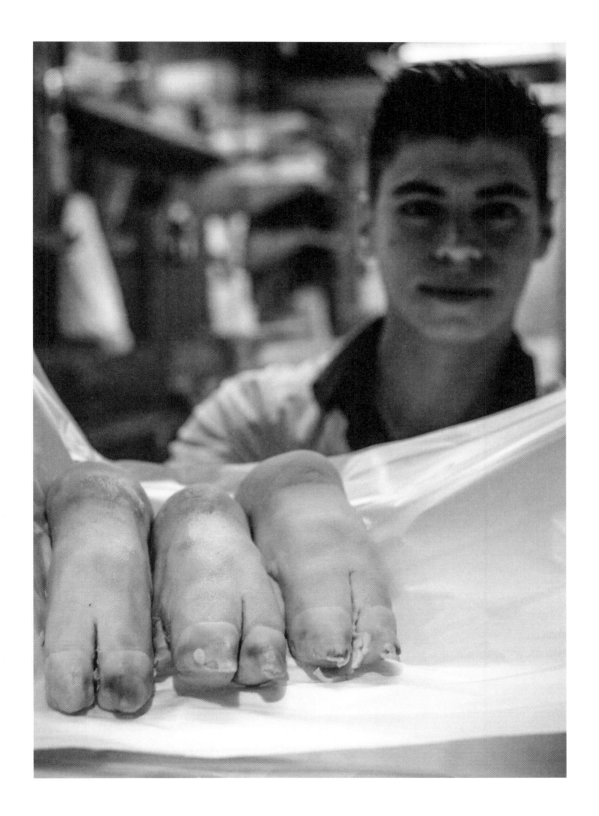

MEAT

POTATO & CHORIZO STEW

This stew from Rioja is simple but you do need to cut the potatoes correctly (into 'cachelos', see boiled octopus, page 156) to ensure that their starch thickens the liquid. Everyone loves this – it's a very wintry, weekend-y, comforting dish. You can't get it wrong. In Spain, every mum makes this.

4 potatoes

240g mild or spicy cooking chorizo

25ml extra virgin olive oil, plus more to serve

1 large Spanish onion, julienned

2 bay leaves

100ml white wine

1 litre chicken stock or water, or a 50/50 mixture of both

sea salt and freshly ground black pepper

2 tablespoons chopped fresh flat-leaf parsley leaves

Peel the potatoes. Partially cut into them, then pull them apart into chunky, uneven-edged pieces around 3cm in size. Cut the chorizo to half the size of the potatoes.

Put the olive oil into a big pan on a medium heat, then add the onion and cook gently for about 15 minutes, without colouring. Add the chorizo and when it starts to caramelize, add the potatoes, bay leaves and wine. Cook until the wine has evaporated, then add the chicken stock and/or water and season.

Half cover the pan with a lid, and continue cooking on a low-medium heat. The more slowly you cook it, the more starch will come out of the potatoes – it should take about 25 minutes. When the potatoes are cooked through, add the chopped parsley.

Serve with a drizzle of olive oil to finish, and bread to dip.

BASQUE BEAN STEW

Tolosa is a town in the Basque country known for its beans, which are black and creamy when cooked. This dish is known as *alubia de Tolosa,* but it's something that's eaten throughout Spain.

This bean and meat stew is a common thing to eat at the weekend, or when family are visiting – it's a celebratory sort of meal. You eat the beans first, then the meat. It's quite rich, so you need the pickled *piparras* to cut through the fattiness, and lots of red wine – and then a siesta afterwards . . .

If you can't find Tolosa beans, you can use good-quality white or black beans instead.

500g dried Tolosa beans, soaked in water overnight

1 onion, peeled and cut in half

1 bay leaf

600g pork ribs

2 medium potatoes, peeled and cut into quarters

300g good-quality smoked pancetta, skin off (in one piece)

4 whole chorizo (around 100–120g each)

3 rice *morcilla* (or the best you can afford), about 150g each

sea salt and freshly ground black pepper

pickled *piparras* or *guindilla* peppers, to serve

Drain the beans, then put them into a large pot or casserole dish with enough fresh water to cover them by one and a half times. This is important: you don't want so much water that the beans will overcook. Throw in the onion, bay leaf and pork ribs, but don't add any salt at this stage – it will make the skins separate from the beans.

Partially cover with the lid and cook on a medium heat, so it's gently bubbling, for 20–25 minutes, then add the potatoes and pancetta.

Add the chorizo and *morcilla* 10–12 minutes before the end (any longer and the *morcilla* will break), with enough water to just cover.

Taste, and when the beans are soft, season.

To serve, everything must be hot (except the pickles). Discard the onion and bay leaf and transfer the potatoes, pork ribs, chorizo, pancetta and *morcilla* to a large plate. Put the *piparras* on a small plate. Slice the chorizo and *morcilla* into medallions and chop the pancetta into lardons. Serve everything in the middle of the table: the beans in their pot, the plate of meat and potatoes, and the pickles, with lots of bread to scoop up the juices.

OXTAIL STEW

Slow-braising is unpredictable: the cooking liquid might reduce to nothing, or you might have perfectly cooked meat, but lots of thin stock. However, it's easy enough to fix. Just add water (not more stock, it will make it too strong-tasting) if you want more sauce or, if it's too liquid, remove the meat, put the pan on the heat and reduce down.

Any leftovers make delicious tempura.

1 oxtail (ask your butcher to cut it into 5cm pieces)

200g plain flour

rapeseed or sunflower oil, for frying

30ml extra virgin olive oil

1 onion, finely diced

4 cloves of garlic, finely sliced

sea salt and freshly ground black pepper

1 leek, finely diced

½ a stick of celery, diced

2 carrots, finely diced

2 bay leaves

1 bottle of red wine

2 litres chicken stock

Dust the oxtail pieces with flour. Put about 3½cm of rapeseed or sunflower oil into a pan on a medium heat. Add the floured oxtail pieces and caramelize until they are crispy and golden brown, then drain on kitchen paper. Preheat the oven to 200°C.

Put the olive oil into an ovenproof pan, large enough to hold the oxtail, and place on a medium heat. Add the onion and garlic with a pinch of salt and allow to caramelize, then add the rest of the vegetables and the bay leaves and cook until very soft. Add the wine and cook until most of it has evaporated, then pour in the chicken stock and bring to the boil. Return the oxtail to the pan, cover with foil, and braise in the oven for 2½ hours, until the oxtail is very soft and the meat is falling off the bone.

Remove the oxtail from the pan. Wait for the cooking liquid to cool slightly, then skim the fat off from the top. Return the pan to the heat and reduce the sauce down until slightly sticky and syrupy, then put the oxtail back into the pan. Serve with mashed potato. Pray that there is some left over.

Note: Leftovers: tempura

Pass the vegetables through a sieve, then reduce the sauce until thick. Break the oxtail into pieces, using your hands. Dip the pieces of oxtail first in flour, then in whisked egg and panko breadcrumbs, and shallow-fry in olive oil. Serve with the sauce, some chilli jam, and with chopped fresh coriander on top.

BEEF STEW

When I'm making a stew, I like to add a lot of root vegetables, like celeriac and swede. That's what makes it taste so homey: the vegetables add an intensity and sweetness, bringing another level of flavour to the stew. This is spoon food, though, for Spanish people; one spoon is their spoon and the other is their piece of bread.

1 onion

½ a celeriac

1 swede

1 carrot

1 leek

4 sticks of celery

1kg good-quality braising beef (ask your butcher what's best)

100ml extra virgin olive oil

6 cloves of garlic, 4 thinly sliced and 2 finely chopped

2 bay leaves

½ a bunch of fresh thyme

1 bottle of red wine

2.5 litres chicken stock

½ a Hispi cabbage

1 small dried Cayenne pepper

sea salt and freshly ground black pepper

Chop the onion and set aside, then chop all the other vegetables (except the cabbage) into big cubes around 2½cm.

Cut the beef into cubes a little bit bigger, around 4 x 4cm.

Put 50ml of olive oil into a large pan on a medium heat. Add the beef and let it caramelize – you may need to do this in batches – until it's golden brown on all sides, then remove from the pan.

Add another 30ml of olive oil to the pan and cook the onions and the sliced garlic until they are translucent, then add the rest of the chopped vegetables (not the cabbage) along with the bay leaves and thyme. Cook gently for a little bit, until the vegetables are starting to take colour, then put the meat back into the pan and add the wine. Cook until the wine has reduced by about half, to evaporate the alcohol. Add the stock, cover the pan tightly with foil and cook on a low-medium heat for 2–2½ hours. (Check on it, and if the liquid has reduced down too much, add more water – you don't need to add more stock.)

Cut the cabbage into 50p-size pieces. Heat the remaining 20ml of olive oil in a separate pan, and fry the cabbage gently with the chopped garlic, Cayenne, salt and pepper.

Spoon the juicy stew into bowls, and serve the cabbage on top.

BAKED AUBERGINE WITH MINCED BEEF & IDIAZABAL CHEESE

FOR 4 (½ AN AUBERGINE PER PERSON)

This is quite a filling dish – it's a classic Mum's recipe, like *pencas* (see page 70). I ate it recently for the first time in many years when I visited a small village near Cádiz that we had to drive for hours through the surrounding mountains to get to. This is my version.

Any leftover meat sauce can be frozen and eaten with pasta another day.

2 aubergines

sea salt and freshly ground black pepper

30ml extra virgin olive oil

300g good-quality minced beef (or use pork or chicken mince)

2 cloves of garlic, chopped

1 onion, chopped

½ a fresh red chilli, chopped

2 carrots, chopped

1 leek, chopped

1 stick of celery, chopped

100ml white wine

1 teaspoon smoked paprika

250g tinned plum tomatoes

2 teaspoons chopped fresh chives

60g unsmoked Idiazabal cheese

Preheat the oven to 160–170°C.

Cut the aubergines in half, then make criss-cross cuts about 1cm deep into the flesh – this will help it to cook through. Season with salt and pepper, rub with olive oil, then place on a baking tray, cover with foil and roast for 30–35 minutes. You want the aubergines to be very soft, but it's important not to burn their skin or they will be tough.

While the aubergines are roasting, put a little oil into a large pan on a medium heat, and cook the minced beef until all the water has evaporated. Once the mince has started to brown a bit, remove it from the pan.

Add the rest of the oil to the pan, then put in the garlic and onions and a little salt. Cook until caramelized, then add the chilli, carrots, leek and celery. Reduce the heat slightly, to medium-low, and cook until the vegetables are soft. Season with salt and pepper, then add the wine. Cook until the wine has evaporated, then add the paprika and tomatoes. Return the meat to the pan and cook everything slowly on a low heat until thick. Stir in the chives.

Heat your grill to hot.

When the aubergines are ready, spoon the meat and sauce mixture on to the aubergine halves. Grate the cheese over the top and put under the grill until melted and crispy. Cut into slices to serve.

CALVES' LIVER, ROCKET & CHILLI

FOR 4

When I was very little, my mum used to make me drink blended calves' liver with milk – it's very healthy, though I didn't know I was having liver at the time!

In this recipe everything is pan-fried very quickly; it only takes 5 minutes but it's full of flavour. You don't want to caramelize the liver because then it will be dry – it should still be juicy inside. Ask your butcher to cut it into ½cm slices for you, then into chunks – it should be similar in width to pappardelle but not so long, otherwise it will be difficult to eat.

150g rocket (or substitute turnip tops or any peppery leaf)

500g calves' liver (prepared as above)

50ml extra virgin olive oil, plus extra to finish

2 shallots, sliced into rings

sea salt and freshly ground black pepper

2 cloves of garlic, finely sliced

1 fresh red chilli, cut in half lengthways, then very thinly sliced into half-rings

4 slices of bread, toasted

Cut the rocket or turnip tops into pieces roughly the same size as the calves' liver.

Heat 25ml of olive oil in a pan and fry the shallots until crispy and golden brown. Set them aside.

Put another pan on a medium-high heat. When it is very hot – almost starting to smoke – add the remaining 25ml of olive oil, salt and pepper (be careful!). Add the garlic, then the calves' liver, and shake the pan. Now add the chilli, then the rocket or turnip tops.

Season again and spoon on to the toast, finishing with an extra drizzle of olive oil and topping with the crispy shallots.

LAMB CUTLETS WITH *TUMBET*

FOR 4

Tumbet is traditional home cooking at its best. I last ate it in Majorca, where it comes from, and was amazed at the simplicity of the peppers, aubergines and potatoes served with the lamb underneath. The restaurant was one of those old places where, even though they had no air-conditioning and it was boiling outside, it felt lovely and cool.

People tend to eat more lamb than pork in Majorca, but *tumbet* topped with a fried egg would also make a great meat-free dinner.

For the *tumbet*

2 large red peppers

1 aubergine, sliced into 1cm rounds

sea salt and freshly ground black pepper

50ml extra virgin olive oil, plus enough for the potatoes

1 potato, sliced into 1cm rounds

spicy tomato sauce (see page 236)

For the lamb

8 lamb cutlets (ask your butcher to French trim these for you)

sea salt and freshly ground black pepper

2 tablespoons *ajillo* (see page 283)

Preheat your oven to 170–180°C.

Roast the peppers in a pan or under the grill. When their skin is completely blistered, put them into a bowl and cover with cling film. Leave to steam, then peel them and remove the seeds while still warm (do this over a bowl to keep all the cooking juices). Strain the juices through a sieve, pushing down on any skin, and reserve.

Season the aubergines with salt and leave in a colander for 10 minutes. Put the olive oil into a large pan on a medium heat. Fry the aubergines until coloured on both sides, then remove and season. Wipe down the pan, then pour in 1cm of olive oil and put the pan back on a medium heat. Add the potatoes and shallow-fry until light gold, soft around the edge but still a little raw in the middle. Season.

Grease a small tray or baking dish with olive oil. Put in all the potatoes in one layer, then add the aubergines, followed by the peppers, seasoning each layer. Cover with the tomato sauce, then roast in the oven for 10–12 minutes, until everything melds together and is cooked through. Season the lamb cutlets with salt and pepper. Put a pan on a medium heat. When hot, add the cutlets and fry until they get a nice golden brown crust then flip them over – 1–1½ minutes per side will give you a medium cutlet.

Drizzle the *ajillo* over the lamb cutlets to finish, and serve with the hot *tumbet* on the side.

PAN-FRIED LAMB SWEETBREADS WITH GARLIC, CHILLI & PARSLEY

FOR 4

A lot of people like to blanch their sweetbreads before frying, but I think you lose flavour this way – and if your sweetbreads are really good quality and fresh, this extra cooking stage isn't necessary.

800g lamb sweetbreads

80ml pomace or light olive oil

sea salt and freshly ground black pepper

20g unsalted butter

2 fresh red chillies, chopped

4 cloves of garlic, crushed

4 tablespoons chopped fresh flat-leaf parsley leaves

100g roast almonds, crushed into large pieces

Remove the white skin from the sweetbreads (this is the fattiest part).

Heat the olive oil in a pan, then add the sweetbreads. They are very delicate and quite milky, so you need to leave them in the pan for 2–3 minutes before turning (if you try to turn them too early they will break up). Season with salt and pepper. When the sweetbreads are caramelized, add the butter and cook until they turn golden and crispy.

Add the chillies, garlic, parsley and almonds. Fry everything for 30 seconds, just to combine, then season and eat straight away with bread.

DESSERTS

My father loves desserts. Whenever our family went out to eat, my dad would always have a classic like *crema catalana*, *cuajada* (see page 262) or *flan* (see page 275) – creamy desserts you eat with a little spoon, that slip down easily.

I tend to be too full for dessert – I'll have one bite, two maximum. I've always been like this about sweet things, though I do love Nutella . . . Sometimes when I go to Spain, especially the south, my girlfriend will have a dessert at the end of lunch or dinner and I'll have a plate of *jamón* and a glass of wine. A plate of ham for dessert: I love that. So it's probably not surprising that my favourite desserts aren't overly sweet.

One of the best, most simple ways to finish a meal is with fruit. My parents were very good about this: we always had a huge basket full of apples, pears, oranges, bananas, and some more exotic fruits like kiwis and mangoes. This is something that's stayed with me, and we often made fruit salad for the staff at Barrafina. Of course, there are other ways to eat fruit too – when it's paired with crisp pastry, even I can be tempted (see cherry tart, pear tart, thin apple tart, pages 270, 272, 279).

Many of these recipes make a good breakfast or go well with a late afternoon cup of coffee or tea: doughnuts and hot chocolate sauce (see page 276) and *torrijas* (see page 258) are two obvious candidates, but *arroz con leche* (see page 256) would make a warming, fragrant start to the day too.

ARROZ CON LECHE

This is a classic dessert. Every mother in Spain knows how to make *arroz con leche*: it's a taste of childhood. Kids love it – but normally eat only about four spoons!

Cooking the rice takes longer than normal because you don't want it to be al dente – it should be soft, with no bite, for a light and creamy pudding. It can be served warm or cold.

1 litre whole milk

1 cinnamon stick

the peel of 1 orange, in a strip

the peel of 1 lemon, in a strip

140g Calasparra or Bomba rice

40g unsalted butter

50ml double cream

160g caster sugar

ground cinnamon, to finish

Put the milk into a pan on a low heat and infuse with the cinnamon and citrus peel until steaming – around 15–18 minutes. The more slowly you steam it, the more flavourful it will be. Turn off the heat and leave to cool, then pass through a sieve.

Wash the rice in cold water to get rid of as much of the starch as possible – the water should run clear.

Add the butter and cream to the infused milk, put back on a low heat and let the butter melt, then add the sugar and cook until dissolved. Add the rice and continue stirring on a low heat for a minimum of 30 minutes, until the rice is cooked and looks creamy. Cooking it on a low heat should keep it liquid – if it starts to dry out a bit, add an extra splash of milk.

Serve warm, dusted with ground cinnamon. If serving cold, leave to come to room temperature, then spoon into glasses or cups, dust generously with ground cinnamon and refrigerate.

TORRIJAS

Usually, you'd use old bread to make *torrijas* – it's what people used to eat when their bread went stale – but I like to use brioche, as it's more buttery and naughtier.

The *crema pastelera* (custard cream) will keep for up to 3 days in the fridge, so you could make it in advance – just whisk together to loosen before using. Any leftover *crema pastelera* can be used to fill doughnuts or to make custard tarts.

½ a loaf of brioche (250g)

250ml whole milk

250ml double cream

1 cinnamon stick

175g caster sugar

1 lemon

a knob of butter, to caramelize (25g-ish)

caster sugar, to sprinkle

For the almond cream

125g toasted almonds, coarsely ground

125g butter

20ml white rum

125g icing sugar

150g *crema pastelera* (see below)

For the *crema pastelera*

500ml whole milk

½ a cinnamon stick

½ a vanilla pod

4 gratings of lemon zest

5 egg yolks

100g caster sugar

60g cornflour

To make the *crema pastelera*, put the milk into a pan on a low heat and infuse with the cinnamon, vanilla and lemon zest until steaming – around 15–18 minutes. Turn off the heat and leave to cool, then pass through a sieve to make a smooth mixture. Whisk the egg yolks with the sugar until pale and creamy and the sugar has dissolved. Add the cornflour and mix again, making sure there are no lumps. Add the infused milk bit by bit, then return to the heat. Cook on a very low heat until it thickens to a béchamel consistency and holds together – around 15–20 minutes, depending on the size of your pan. Set aside.

Cut the crusts off the brioche, then cut into thick (3cm) slices and cut these in half – you should have 3cm x 3cm chunks. Infuse the milk and cream with the cinnamon, sugar and lemon – heat slightly to dissolve the sugar – then leave to cool. Put the bread into a container in a single layer and pour over the infused milk. Cover with cling film and leave in the fridge overnight.

To make the almond cream, put the toasted almonds, butter and rum into a pan on a medium heat. When the rum starts to bubble, mix in the icing sugar. Leave to cool slightly, then fold in 150g of the *crema pastelera*.

Put the butter into a frying pan on a medium heat. When it's melted, sprinkle over a little sugar, then add the brioche to the pan (it should have soaked up the milk). Caramelize all sides of the brioche pieces until golden brown, sprinkling with more sugar as you turn them – they should be crispy outside but milky within.

Spoon the almond cream on to a plate, and put the *torrijas* on top – serve as is, or with ice cream.

GOXUA

Goxua means 'sweet' in Basque. This is a classic, old-fashioned dessert: the recipe comes from Maria Begoña Luis, the mother of one of my chefs, Urko, at Barrafina Drury Lane.

caster sugar, for sprinkling

For the whipped vanilla cream

250ml double cream

40g caster sugar

1 vanilla pod, split

zest of 1 lime

For the *crema pastelera*

150ml whole milk

1 cinnamon stick

1 vanilla pod, split

zest of ½ an orange

zest of ½ a lemon

4 egg yolks

150g caster sugar

40g cornflour

For the sponge

4 eggs

120g caster sugar

120g plain flour

For the rum syrup

100g sugar

100ml water

50ml good-quality black rum

Utensils

4 metal ramekin rings approximately 7cm in size

Whip all the ingredients for the vanilla cream until it holds together without being stiff. Refrigerate for about 2 hours, until set.

To make the *crema pastelera*, put the milk into a pan on a low heat and infuse with the cinnamon, vanilla and zest until steaming – around 15–18 minutes. Turn off the heat and leave to cool, then pass through a sieve to make a smooth mixture. Whisk the egg yolks with the sugar until pale and creamy and the sugar has dissolved. Add the cornflour and mix again, making sure there are no lumps. Add the infused milk bit by bit, then return to the heat. Cook on a very low heat until it thickens to a béchamel consistency – around 15–20 minutes, depending on the size of your pan. Leave to cool, then refrigerate.

For the sponge, preheat the oven to 180°C. Beat the eggs and sugar together until tripled in size. Sieve the flour, then fold it into the eggs and sugar gently with a spatula. Pour into a baking tin (A3 size) and bake for about 12 minutes [check], until golden brown. Make sure it's cooked by inserting a toothpick and checking it comes out clean.

To make the rum syrup, put the sugar and water into a pan on a medium heat until dissolved – about 5–7 minutes. When it becomes syrupy, add the rum. You want it to be able to coat the back of a spoon.

Brush the sponge with the rum syrup until drunk – we call this '*borracho*'. You want a very drunk, sticky sponge!

Use your ramekin rings to cut out the sponge, and place on plates. Add 1cm of whipped vanilla cream to each one, then another drunk sponge, then 2cm of *crema pastelera*. Sprinkle with the caster sugar and burn with a blowtorch.

LECHE FRITA

Perfect for breakfast, brunch or at teatime, *leche frita* is best when eaten warm, fresh from the pan – the custard should explode in your mouth like a little bomb – but any leftovers are nice cold too.

You can make the orange sauce in advance and keep it in the fridge for up to a week. It can be served hot or cold.

rapeseed or sunflower oil, for shallow-frying

plain flour, for dusting

1 egg, whisked

icing sugar, to finish

For the *leche frita*

500ml whole milk

zest of 1 lemon

1 cinnamon stick

1 egg

4 medium egg yolks

100g caster sugar

40g cornflour

For the orange sauce

1 orange (preferably Seville)

40g caster sugar

20ml water

50g Ponche Caballero (or use Cointreau)

1 cinnamon stick

Peel the orange without including any of the pith, then cut the peel into shreds. Divide the orange into segments and remove the membrane and any remaining pith. Put the orange peel and segments into a pan on a low-medium heat with the rest of the ingredients for the orange sauce, and stir together gently. It will start to break down and become almost like marmalade. Cook for around 15 minutes, continuing to stir – add a splash more water if it looks like it needs it. It should be thick but not too runny.

To make the *leche frita*, put the milk into a saucepan on a low heat with the lemon zest and cinnamon, and infuse until steaming. Pass the milk through a sieve.

Off the heat, put the egg and egg yolks into a separate pan (a sauté or other high-sided pan, as you are going to be whisking the sauce in it) and whisk together. Add the sugar and whisk together until fluffy and billowing, then add the cornflour. Add the milk to the egg mix slowly, bit by bit, then place on a very low heat for around 12–15 minutes. You have to keep stirring – if you leave it for a minute it will burn underneath, so you need to make sure it's moving.

Line a container with cling film, leaving enough overlap to wrap round. Pour in the milk and egg mix, wrap the cling film over the top (covering it), and leave it in the fridge until you can touch it with your finger and feel that it's squidgy – like jelly but not. You can do this the day before. The next day, or 5–6 hours later, remove the cling film and you will have a block of *leche frita*. Slice, then cut into pieces around 3cm x 2cm.

Put the oil into a pan on a medium heat. Flour and egg-wash the pieces of *leche frita*, then shallow-fry for 30–40 seconds, turning them over once. It will be very creamy and almost melting inside.

Spoon the orange sauce on to plates and top with the *leche frita*. Sprinkle with icing sugar and serve.

CUAJADA

My father would always eat this if we went out to a restaurant: as he soon as he heard the word '*cuajada*' he wouldn't need to hear anything else! Traditionally, it's made with just goat's milk and rennet, though my version has cream cheese and sugar too. It's a really easy dessert to make, especially if you already have dry rennet at home: you can't mess it up.

250ml whole milk

250ml single cream

65g caster sugar

125g full fat cream cheese

12g *cuajo* (dry rennet, used to curdle cheese)

honey, to serve

toasted hazelnuts or walnuts, broken up, to serve

Put the milk, cream, sugar and cream cheese into a pan on a low-medium heat, until just melted – you don't want it to steam. Stir, then add the rennet and whisk together so it's not lumpy – it will start to thicken. Ladle into small glasses or cups and put into the fridge until it sets – a minimum of 3 hours.

Serve with honey and toasted hazelnuts on top.

PEACHES IN SYRUP

Open the cupboard in any kitchen in Spain and you'll find tinned fruit in syrup – it's an instant dessert. This is my version – it's a lovely way to eat peaches and really simple. Ideally, you want peaches that are ripe but not too ripe, otherwise they will fall apart when you cook them.

6 nice white peaches

1 litre water

1kg caster sugar

½ a bunch of fresh lemon verbena, leaves picked

clotted cream, to serve

Cut the peaches in half and remove the stones.

To make the syrup, put the water, sugar and lemon verbena into a pan and bring to a gentle boil for 5 minutes. Add the halved peaches and cook for around 12 minutes (depending on your peaches). Take off the heat and allow to cool a little, then take the skins off the peaches. Transfer the fruit to a container and leave for a couple of hours, until the syrup starts to take on the colour of the peaches.

Serve with clotted cream – you can spoon this into the peach cavities – and the syrup.

ORANGE SORBET

Use whatever oranges are in season – blood oranges are great in winter. Before you mix everything together, taste the juice to see how sweet it is – you might need to reduce the sugar by half, depending on your oranges.

8 oranges

600ml orange juice (from the oranges – see method)

250ml water

360g caster sugar

40g glucose

juice of 1 lemon

Trim the base off each orange so it will sit flat, then cut off the top (keep these). Scoop out the middle, then mash through a sieve with the back of a spoon to get all the juice out. Depending on how juicy your oranges are, you may need a few extra. Put the orange shells into the freezer so they're nice and cold.

Put the water, sugar and glucose into a pan and bring to the boil, stirring to help the sugar dissolve. Leave to cool, then add the orange and lemon juice.

Churn in an ice cream machine until smooth and creamy.

Fill the frozen oranges with the sorbet and close with the reserved tops of the oranges. Put back into the freezer for another 5 minutes or so, just to freeze the tops on.

LEMON SORBET

Sorbet should always be sharp: you should taste the acidity of the lemon first, and then the sugar to balance it. Lemons vary in juiciness, so always buy a few extra.

When I was a child, this is how sorbets would always be served.

10 unwaxed lemons

600ml lemon juice (from the lemons – see method)

250ml water

360g caster sugar

40g glucose

juice of 2 limes

Trim the base off each lemon so it will sit flat, then cut off the top (keep these). Scoop out the middle, then mash through a sieve with the back of a spoon to get all the juice out. Depending on how juicy your lemons are, you may need a few extra. Put the lemon shells into the freezer so they're nice and cold.

Put the water, sugar and glucose into a pan and bring to the boil, stirring to help the sugar dissolve. Leave to cool, then add the lemon and lime juice.

Churn in an ice cream machine until smooth and creamy.

Fill the frozen lemons with the sorbet and close with the reserved tops of the lemons. Put back into the freezer for another 5 minutes or so, just to freeze the tops on.

WALNUT & SULTANA ICE CREAM
IN PX SHERRY

MAKES AROUND 1 LITRE

I like ice cream to have a bit of texture – here you have soaked sultanas and walnut pieces. PX wine adds a warm, oaky flavour: you know it's going to be good.

200g sultanas

Pedro Ximénez (PX) sherry, enough to cover the sultanas

10 egg yolks

200g caster sugar

1 litre whole milk

200ml double cream

200g walnuts, lightly roasted

Cover the sultanas with the PX sherry and leave to soak overnight.

Whisk the egg yolks and sugar together until pale and creamy and the sugar has dissolved.

Put the milk, double cream and roasted walnuts into a pan on a low heat until just steaming – the walnuts will break down and flavour the milk. Slowly add to the egg yolks and sugar bit by bit, whisking it together. Pour back into the pan and put on a low-medium heat. Keep stirring – don't go anywhere! – and cook until the temperature measures 83–85°C on a kitchen thermometer (until the eggs are cooked and the mixture looks thick).

Pour into a container and cool in the fridge for a few hours, then put into an ice cream machine and churn until smooth and creamy – 5 minutes before this point, when the paddle can still just turn, add the sultanas and sherry.

TURRÓN ICE CREAM
WITH ALAMEDA SHERRY

MAKES AROUND 1 LITRE

If you go to any Spanish shop you'll find at least three or four types of *turrón* (nougat): almond and caramel (hard), almond, egg and sugar (soft), and chocolate and egg yolk.

Turrón is usually eaten at Christmas – we always have a full basket of dried fruit, *turrón* and *polvorones* (Spanish shortbread).

1 hard tablet and ¼ of a soft tablet of *turrón*

10 egg yolks

200g caster sugar

1 litre double cream

Alameda sherry, to pour over the ice cream

Blend the *turrón* in a food processor until crumbly. You don't want it completely smooth – it should still have some texture.

Whisk the egg yolks and sugar together until pale and creamy and the sugar has dissolved.

Put the double cream into a pan on a low heat until steaming. Slowly add to the egg yolks and sugar bit by bit, whisking together. Add three-quarters of the blended *turrón*, breaking it up further as you mix it together. Pour back into the pan and put on a low-medium heat. Keep stirring – don't go anywhere! – and cook until the temperature reaches 83–85°C on a kitchen thermometer (until the eggs are cooked and the mixture looks thick).

Pour into a container and cool in the fridge for a few hours, then put into an ice cream machine and churn until smooth and creamy – 5 minutes before this point, when the paddle can still just turn, add the reserved quarter of *turrón*.

Serve with Alameda sherry poured over – as much as you like!

CHERRY TART

When I first came to London, you couldn't find good cherries; my butcher used to bring me a box of large, burgundy cherries from Spain every year and when he did, I would make this tart.

This recipe makes enough for two pastry tarts but you can always freeze one half – or make the pear tart on page 272.

1kg of the best possible dark red cherries, halved and pitted

150ml *orujo* (Galician spirit, like grappa)

icing sugar, to finish

For the sweet pastry

420g cold but malleable butter, cut into cubes, plus extra to grease the tin

300g icing sugar

750g flour, plus extra to dust

30g ground almonds (or blended whole almonds)

2 eggs

2 egg yolks

zest of 3 lemons

3 vanilla pods

For the *crema pastelera*

500ml whole milk

½ a cinnamon stick

½ a vanilla pod

zest of 1 lemon

5 egg yolks

100g caster sugar

60g cornflour

Leave the cherries to soak in the *orujo* for 6–8 hours or overnight, then drain (reserving the *orujo*).

To make the sweet pastry, mix the ingredients in a food processor or by hand until they come together. Divide into two flat balls, wrap in cling film and refrigerate.

To make the *crema pastelera*, put the milk into a pan on a low heat and infuse with the cinnamon, vanilla and lemon zest until steaming – around 15–18 minutes. Turn off the heat and leave to cool, then pass through a sieve to make a smooth mixture. Whisk the egg yolks with the sugar until pale and creamy and the sugar has dissolved. Add the cornflour and mix again, making sure there are no lumps. Add the infused milk bit by bit, then return to the heat. Cook on a very low heat until it thickens to a béchamel consistency and holds together – around 15–20 minutes, depending on the size of your pan.

Preheat your oven to 180°C, and grease a tart tin (26cm, with a removable bottom) with a little butter.

Flour a sheet of baking paper and place it on a work surface somewhere cool. Remove one ball of pastry from the fridge, place it on the baking paper, and roll it out as quickly as possible to a circle at least 4cm bigger than your tin and around 3mm thick. If your pastry gets too warm and starts to melt you can put it back into the fridge to cool down.

Put your hand underneath the baking paper and gently turn the pastry out into the tin, then mould it into shape, making sure the sides are 90°. Trim the sides but leave ½cm extra, as it will shrink when it bakes: you can shape it later. Prick the base all over with a fork to help it cook through and not puff up. Put it back into the fridge for 5–10 minutes, or until it's cold (otherwise the butter may melt too quickly when it goes into the oven).

Bake for 15–20 minutes, keeping an eye on it and turning it so it cooks evenly. When nice and golden, leave to cool down then fill it halfway up with the cooled *crema*. Put it back into the fridge for 20–30 minutes to set, then remove and place the cherries cut side down over the *crema* until it's completely covered.

Put the *orujo* into a pan and reduce until syrupy, then brush over the cherries and dust with icing sugar before serving.

PEAR TART

The perfect use for the extra pastry case left over from making the cherry tart (see page 270).

8 not overly ripe pears

175g butter

60g caster sugar

icing sugar, to finish

For the sweet pastry

420g cold but malleable butter, cut into cubes, plus extra to grease the tin

300g icing sugar

750g flour, plus extra to dust

30g ground almonds (or blended whole almonds)

2 eggs

2 egg yolks

zest of 3 lemons

3 vanilla pods

For the *crema pastelera*

500ml whole milk

½ a cinnamon stick

½ a vanilla pod

zest of 1 lemon

5 egg yolks

100g caster sugar

60g cornflour

To make the sweet pastry, mix the ingredients in a food processor or by hand until they come together. Divide into two flat balls, wrap in cling film and refrigerate.

To make the *crema pastelera*, put the milk into a pan on a low heat and infuse with the cinnamon, vanilla and lemon zest until steaming – around 15–18 minutes. Turn off the heat and leave to cool, then pass through a sieve to make a smooth mixture. Whisk the egg yolks with the sugar until pale and creamy and the sugar has dissolved. Add the cornflour and mix again, making sure there are no lumps. Add the infused milk bit by bit, then return to the heat. Cook on a very low heat until it thickens to a béchamel consistency and holds together – around 15–20 minutes, depending on the size of your pan.

Peel the pears, cut them into quarters and remove the core. Put them into a large, flat pan with the butter and sugar and place on a medium-low heat. Cook for 15–20 minutes, until everything melts together and they caramelize, then remove from the heat.

Preheat your oven to 180°C and grease a tart tin (26cm, with a removable bottom) with a little butter.

Flour a sheet of baking paper and place it on a work surface somewhere cool. Remove one ball of pastry from the fridge, place it on the baking paper, and roll it out as quickly as possible to a circle at least 4cm bigger than your tin and around 3mm thick. If your pastry gets too warm and starts to melt, you can put it back into the fridge to cool down.

Put your hand underneath the baking paper and gently turn the pastry out into the tin, then mould it into shape, making sure the sides are 90°. Trim the sides but leave ½cm extra, as it will shrink when it bakes:

you can shape it later. Prick the base all over with a fork to help it cook through and not puff up. Put it back into the fridge for 5–10 minutes or until it is cold (otherwise the butter may melt too quickly when it goes into the oven).

Bake for 15–20 minutes, keeping an eye on it and turning it so it cooks evenly. When nice and golden, leave to cool down, then fill it halfway up with the cooled *crema*. Put it back into the fridge for 20–30 minutes to set. Place the pear pieces on top of the *crema* until it's completely covered, and dust with icing sugar before serving.

FLAN

In a good *flan* the caramel should be dark to offset the sweetness, so you need to leave it slightly longer than you normally would – but not too long, or it will burn!

The traditional way to eat *flan* is with whipped cream and walnuts on the side.

For the custard

250ml whole milk

125 double cream

125g single cream

1 vanilla pod, split

4 eggs

2 egg yolks

150g caster sugar

For the caramel

200ml water

125g caster sugar

To serve

whipped cream

walnuts

To make the caramel, put the water and caster sugar into a pan and put it on a medium heat. Cook until it melts and forms a dark golden-brown caramel. Don't go anywhere while this is happening. Pour ½cm of caramel into each of six ramekins and leave to cool down.

Put the milk into a pan on a low heat with the double and single creams and the split vanilla pod and leave to infuse. Don't let it boil.

Whisk the eggs and egg yolks with the sugar until pale and creamy and the sugar has dissolved. Add the infused milk bit by bit, then pour into the ramekins.

Heat the oven to 160–170°C. Stand the ramekins in a deep roasting tray, then pour hot water into the tray to come halfway up the sides of the ramekins and make a bain-marie. Cover with a flat tray or foil, to stop the tops from colouring. Cook for 18–20 minutes: check it's cooked by taking out one of the ramekins and giving it a little push. The *flan* should wobble but hold together. If it's still loose, give it another 4–5 minutes but keep an eye on it: if the *flan* comes away from the ramekin edge, it's overcooked.

Leave to cool, then refrigerate – it will need 3–4 hours to become cold and set properly. To turn out, fill a bowl with some warm/hot water and dip a ramekin in it for a couple of seconds. Press around the *flan* with your fingers, or cut round it with a small sharp knife to loosen. Invert the ramekin tightly on to a plate and give it a swift sharp shake to the side: you want to hear a 'bloop' kind of sound, indicating that it's come out – like turning out a jelly.

DOUGHNUTS & HOT CHOCOLATE SAUCE

MAKES 20 DOUGHNUTS

This is like an easier version of *churros* with chocolate sauce. If you don't have a mixer to make the dough, you can knead it by hand.

rapeseed or sunflower oil, enough to fill your pan to about 3cm

For the doughnuts

60g cold but malleable butter

450g plain flour, plus extra to dust

60g caster sugar

60ml whole milk

12g fresh yeast or 4g quick yeast

4 eggs

For the hot chocolate sauce

300ml water

150g caster sugar

160ml single cream

50g cocoa powder

300g dark chocolate (70%)

For the cinnamon sugar

150g caster sugar

50–60g ground cinnamon

Take the butter out of the fridge 15 minutes before starting and chop into small cubes.

Put the flour and sugar into a large bowl and mix together with your hands.

Heat the milk until almost steaming, then remove from the heat and leave to cool slightly. Mix into the yeast, stirring with a whisk to dissolve.

Put the flour and sugar into the bowl of a stand mixer and slowly add the butter – it will look like crumble. Add the eggs one by one, then dribble in the milk/yeast mixture until everything comes together into a sticky dough.

Slightly flour a large container or bowl, turn the dough out into it, and lightly flour the top. Cover and leave in the fridge overnight.

In the morning, turn out the dough on to a floured surface – it will have almost doubled. Take a piece (approx. 30g) and roll it in your hands, then squeeze down until it's about 2½cm thick. Use the top of a miniature bottle to press out the dough in the middle, leaving a hole. The doughnuts should be around 25g each. Repeat until you've used up all the dough.

Stick two fingers through the middle of each doughnut and roll them around to push out the dough a bit more and double the size of the hole – otherwise it will close up when the doughnut is fried and expands.

To make the hot chocolate sauce, put the water, sugar and cream into a pan on a low heat and dissolve the sugar. Put the cocoa powder and chocolate into a bowl and place over a pan of simmering water to melt the chocolate (this keeps it smooth). When the chocolate has all melted, add it to the cream with a spatula. Continue mixing until it becomes dense and thick and perfect for dipping. Keep warm.

Mix together the sugar and cinnamon.

Put the oil into a shallow pan on a medium heat. When it's hot, fry the doughnuts until golden brown, then remove and drain on kitchen paper. Dust with the cinnamon sugar while still warm and serve with the chocolate sauce for dipping.

MIXED BERRIES WITH MASCARPONE MOUSSE

When I was a little girl I used to take my bicycle and go all around the countryside looking for different kinds of berries. I guess this is where my passion for them started.

60ml orange-infused olive oil (see page 293)

1 punnet (around 250g) of strawberries, tops removed, cut in half if very large

1 punnet (around 200g) of blueberries

1 punnet (around 200g) of raspberries

the smallest basil leaves, picked, to finish

For the mascarpone mousse

1 egg yolk

50g caster sugar

170ml double cream

220g mascarpone

40ml good whisky, to taste

To make the mousse, whisk the egg yolk and sugar together until pale and creamy, then add the double cream and whisk together until you have soft peaks. Fold in the mascarpone and whisky, then refrigerate to set slightly.

Drizzle the orange olive oil over the berries and mix together very gently.

Spoon the mousse on to plates, then add the berries. Finish with the basil leaves.

278   DESSERTS

THIN APPLE TART

This is the kind of dessert I really like: very thin pastry with glazed, caramelized fruit. It's the perfect thing to pick up and eat with a coffee. If you have the pastry in the freezer already (don't make your own puff pastry unless you're crazy), all you really need is three ingredients.

flour, for dusting

250g puff pastry

4 Granny Smith apples

200g caster sugar

150g cold unsalted butter

50ml Calvados

icing sugar

Preheat the oven to 180°C.

Flour your work surface lightly. Roll the pastry out into a rectangle approx. 22cm long x 6cm wide (and around 2mm thick) – the same width, more or less, as the apple slices when you cut them. Crimp the edges of the pastry with your fingers, and prick the base with a fork to help it cook evenly.

Line a tray with baking paper and place the pastry on top.

Peel the apples, cut them in half and remove the core. Then slice each apple very thinly – around 2mm – not paper-thin, it still needs some texture. Place each whole sliced apple half on the pastry, cut side down, and push down on it so that the apple slices fan out slightly on an angle while still overlapping closely. Sprinkle the sugar over the top. Chop the butter into small cubes and sprinkle over the tart too.

Bake in the oven for 20 minutes. Pour the Calvados on top of the apples, then turn the tart over (use a spatula, or place another lined tray on top and use it to help you turn) to caramelize the apples. Turn the heat down to around 120–130°C and cook for another 10–15 or even 20 minutes until all the pastry is golden brown. Turn it over again, leave to rest for about 10–15 minutes, then sprinkle with icing sugar and serve with ice cream on top, or with coffee on the side. (It's nice to eat it warm, rather than straight from the oven.)

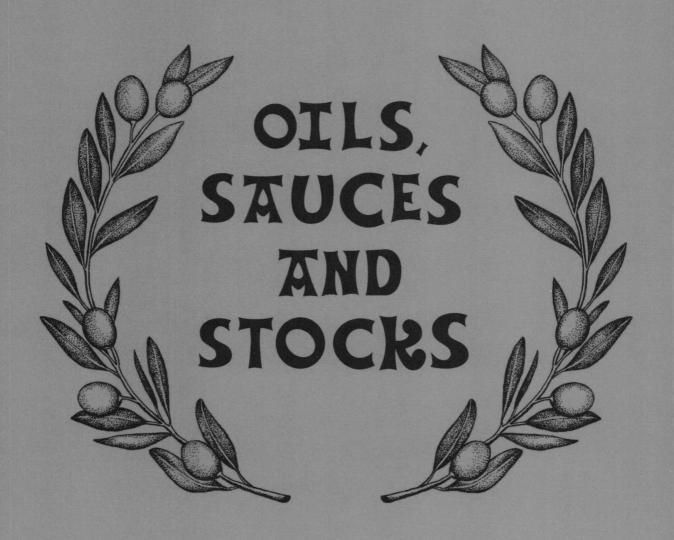

OILS, SAUCES AND STOCKS

AJILLO

My mum used to make this garlic and parsley oil in a pestle and mortar. I couldn't live without my magic oil – it gives me so much confidence. Sometimes you taste a dish and think that it needs an extra something, then you add this and it tastes ten times better. It keeps for 2 or 3 days in the fridge – leave it to come up to room temperature before using.

4 cloves of garlic, very finely chopped

4 tablespoons very finely chopped fresh flat-leaf parsley leaves

200ml extra virgin olive oil

Mix everything together until the oil starts to turn slightly green from the parsley.

SPICY TOMATO (BRAVA) SAUCE

MAKES 1 KG

Chillies differ in spiciness, but you can always add an extra teaspoon of cayenne pepper after blending if you want.

8 dried chillies

250ml extra virgin olive oil

4 cloves of garlic, sliced

2 carrots, finely chopped

3 shallots, finely chopped

1 leek, finely chopped

1 bay leaf

sea salt and freshly ground black pepper

1kg tinned plum tomatoes, blended

caster sugar, to taste (around 1 tablespoon)

Soak the chillies in water, then cut into thin rings (keeping the seeds).

Put the olive oil, garlic and chillies into a pan on a medium-low heat, and cook to make a spicy oil – around 5 minutes. Add all the finely chopped vegetables and the bay leaf with a little pinch of salt, and cook down until really soft and mushy – around 6–8 minutes. Add the blended tomatoes and cook on a medium heat for 30–40 minutes, stirring.

Blend together and season to taste – you might need to add some sugar, or to up the spice. Or, if you think it needs cooking a little longer, to put it back on the heat.

CHILLI OIL

MAKES A SMALL JAR

This is smoky and only a little spicy. Like the *ajillo*, this lifts the flavour of whatever it's added to in a subtle way.

200ml extra virgin olive oil

200g dried *guindilla* chillies, soaked in water, then finely chopped

Mix the oil and chillies together until the oil starts to turn red.

ALIOLI

If you want to make quince *alioli*, cut 150g of quince jelly or quince paste into chunks and melt gently in a bain-marie, then mix into the *alioli* and season.

I always use a mix of oils when I make *alioli*. I don't like it to be too oily and yellow – this is lighter.

3 heads of garlic, plus 1 clove

200ml extra virgin olive oil, plus more for roasting the garlic

sea salt and freshly ground black pepper

1 egg

2 egg yolks

300ml pomace or light olive oil

juice of 1 or 1½ lemons (depending on their juiciness)

Preheat the oven to 170–180°C. Take the 3 heads of garlic and slice crossways a quarter of the way down from the top. Place on a large piece of foil with a drizzle of olive oil, season with salt and pepper, then close the foil. Roast for 20 minutes, until very soft, then squeeze out all the cloves.

Put the roasted garlic into a food processor with the raw garlic clove and blend. Add the egg and yolks one by one, then the olive oil and lemon juice. Season with salt and pepper.

MAYONNAISE

Using a whole egg gives more body to the mayonnaise.

1 egg

2 egg yolks

juice of ½ a lemon

250ml extra virgin olive oil

250ml pomace or light olive oil

sea salt and freshly ground black pepper

Whisk together the egg and yolks, then whisk in the lemon juice. Slowly, bit by bit, add the olive oil, continuing to whisk. When the mixture starts to emulsify you can add the oil a little faster. Season to taste at the end.

CRAB/PRAWN STOCK

MAKES AROUND 500ML

There is nothing intimidating about making stock – it takes 20 minutes, and part of having fun in the kitchen is making things yourself. You can make the stock in advance and freeze it.

30ml extra virgin olive oil

500g small velvet crabs and/or shell-on prawns

1 bay leaf

1 stick of celery, diced

1 medium leek, diced

2 carrots, diced

½ an onion, diced

3 cloves of garlic, crushed

2 tablespoons tomato purée

200ml brandy

2 litres water

Put the olive oil into a large pan, then add the crabs and/or prawns and cook, squashing them down to release their juices. Add the bay leaf, vegetables and garlic and cook until they are really soft. Add the tomato purée and cook for a couple of minutes, then add the brandy and cook to evaporate the alcohol.

At this point, add the water to the pan. Cook for around 20 minutes, then pass through a sieve and leave to rest.

SUPPLIERS

In the same way that my mum used to make sure she got the freshest fish and ripest fruit when shopping at the market, finding the best-quality ingredients is very important to me. I have built up a number of trusted suppliers that I use. Most, though not all, of these companies only supply wholesale, but I'd like to mention them briefly – I've also included a list of shops and websites where you can find many of the ingredients mentioned in the recipes in this book.

Wherever you live, it's important to shop from companies or people you trust, if you can, and to build up a relationship with them. Then, when you need to find something slightly out of the ordinary, you can ask them to help you out, as I do with my suppliers.

BRINDISA (*wholesale and retail, brindisa.com*)

I've been working with Brindisa for the last sixteen years; they are friends of mine and we are very supportive of each other. They were the first company to introduce many Spanish products to the UK, and everything they sell is good quality.

MASH PURVEYORS (*wholesale; retail at New Covent Garden Market, or online, in London, from farmdrop.co.uk, selected produce only***)**

Dating back over 150 years, Mash supply fruit and vegetables to top UK restaurants. They come to see me once a month with a small box of stuff and they always have something I've never seen before – finger limes from Australia, say – which teaches me about new ingredients. Their produce is very fresh, good value and they're lovely people to deal with.

NATOORA (*wholesale, natoora.co.uk; retail from their two London shops and other outlets, or from ocado.co.uk*)

Natoora specialize in Italian produce and have amazing pomegranates with deep burgundy insides, peppers and tomatoes.

IBERFLAVOURS (*wholesale, or check website, iberflavours.com, for smaller retail orders*)

Based in Barcelona, this website delivers amazing Spanish products and many things that are very difficult to get hold of in London (Iberian ribs, pig's ears, top-quality prawns, to name a few).

LE MARCHÉ DES CHEFS (*lemarchedeschefs.co.uk*)

A very small supplier, Maurice is English but grew up in France and travels between London, France and Spain a lot. He is one of the best fresh suppliers I've ever met and has incredible offal, meat and vegetables.

CHANNEL FISHERIES (*wholesale only: channelfisheries.com*)

Brilliant for English fish: they call me in the morning, tell me what the best catch of the day is, I buy it and it's delivered.

BASCO (*wholesale and retail, bascofinefoods.com*)

Run by Javier De La Hormaza, a chef and importer, this company supplies Basque ingredients such as gernikas, piparras, and much more.

OTHER SUPPLIERS, BY INGREDIENT

OILS & VINEGARS

Arbequina olive oil
www.brindisa.com

Arbequina olive oil
with Valencia oranges
www.souschef.co.uk

Moscatel and Pedro Ximénez
(PX) balsamic vinegar
www.brindisa.com

VEGETABLES, PULSES & DRIED CHILLIES

Piperras
www.abelandcole.co.uk

Guindilla chillies
www.brindisa.com

Judión beans
www.brindisa.com
www.souschef.co.uk

CHEESE, OLIVES & NUTS

Idiazabal cheese
www.lafromagerie.co.uk

Rennet
www.cheesemakingshop.co.uk/
Natural-Rennet

Manzanilla olives
www.brindisa.com
www.souschef.co.uk

Marcona almonds
www.brindisa.com
www.souschef.co.uk

STORE CUPBOARD

Soft and hard *turrón*
www.souschef.co.uk

Piquillo peppers
(Navarrico are the best kind)
www.brindisa.com
www.souschef.co.uk

Ortiz bonito and anchovies
www.souschef.co.uk

MEAT & FISH

www.brindisa.com

Chistorra
www.ultracomida.co.uk
www.waitrose.com

Sobrasada
www.sainsburys.co.uk
www.brindisa.com
www.ultracomida.co.uk

Spider crabs
W. Harvey & Sons: www.crabmeat.co.uk

Iberian pork ribs
Tom Hixson: www.tomhixson.co.uk

Jamón

Cinco Jotas
www.cincojotas.com

Anchovies

Don Bocarte
www.donbocarte.com

INDEX

A

adobo: chickpeas, prawns & squid in *adobo* 158

    pork loin in *adobo* & béchamel sauce with broken potatoes 234

ajillo 283

    grilled razor clams *al ajillo* 180

ajo blanco: beetroot salad with *ajo blanco* & dill vinaigrette 102

    mojama, ajo blanco & mango dressing 106

Alameda: *turrón* ice cream with Alameda sherry 269

alioli 287

    alioli cod & potato gratin with sultanas 189

almonds: beetroot salad with *ajo blanco* & dill vinaigrette 102

    cauliflower with salted almonds, shallot & chilli 126

    a feast of calçots with *romesco* 56–7

    Medjool date, almond & smoked pancetta bonbons 37

    mojama, ajo blanco & mango dressing 106

    torrijas 258

anchovies 16, 22

    banderillas 36

    chicory, anchovy & *salmorejo* salad 105

    salted anchovies & lardo on toast 47

    squid, puntarelle, tomatoes, anchovies & capers 142

apples: thin apple tart 279

arroz con leche 256

artichokes: clams & artichokes 168–9

    pan-fried artichokes & *jamón* 52

    see also Jerusalem artichokes

asparagus: baby vegetable salad 107

    green asparagus, *romesco* & Idiazabal cheese 138

aubergines: baked aubergine with minced beef & Idiazabal cheese 248

    cuttlefish & *samfaina* 159

    escalivada 137

    lamb cutlets with *tumbet* 251

avocados: tomato, fennel & avocado salad 99

B

banderillas 36

Basque bean stew 244

beans: Basque bean stew 244

    coco beans & clams 174

    flat green bean, tomato & potato stew 125

    judión & fennel salad with smoked salmon 100

béchamel sauce: pork loin in *adobo* & béchamel sauce with broken potatoes 234

beef: baked aubergine with minced beef & Idiazabal cheese 248

    beef stew 247

    pencas 70

beetroot salad with *ajo blanco* & dill vinaigrette 102

black pudding *see morcilla*

blueberries: mixed berries with mascarpone mousse 278

bonito: *marmitako* 198

bottarga: gem salad with bottarga, walnuts & pine nut dressing 108

bread: beetroot salad with *ajo blanco* & dill vinaigrette 102

    chicory, anchovy & *salmorejo* salad 105

    migas 92

    mojama, ajo blanco & mango dressing 106

    persimmon, goat's cheese & land cress salad 97

    torrijas 258

    see also toast

bream: grilled bream 197

brill: whole brill with garlic sauce 190

brioche: *torrijas* 258

butifarra: *butifarra*, caramelized onions & sherry 235

    stuffed *piquillo* peppers with *butifarra*, prawns & mushrooms 34

C

cabbage: braised Hispi cabbage with garlic cream sauce 122

calçots 56

    calçots in tempura 53

    a feast of calçots with *romesco* 56–7

calves' liver, rocket, chilli 249

capers: squid, puntarelle, tomatoes, anchovies & capers 142

GRACIAS

I could not have written this book without my parents, whose support and love made all the tough moments easier to bear: this book is dedicated to them. I must especially thank my mother, from whom I learned all I know and who made me passionate about cooking. I also thank my brother Pedro and his family (and thanks to him especially for letting us shoot some of the book at his hotel, the Hotel Palacio Muñatones in Muskiz, near my home in Santurtzi).

Many thanks to my beautiful girlfriend, Natalia, who is always beside me, supportive and amazing!

I would like to thank Sam and Eddie Hart, who trusted me to steer the Barrafina ship over the last fourteen years and who have never been afraid to let me experiment. A big thank you to all the team, past and present, at all the branches of Barrafina, who became my second family and made London my home, in particular to Gisela Fernandez for helping me through the process of making this book and being such a good worker and friend; to Diego Garcia who is an exceptional chef and an even better person and who was always there making my job easier; and to Jose Etura, a real partner in crime and always there when I needed him.

Sophie Missing has helped me to write this book: thank you, Sophie, for listening to me and interpreting and then brilliantly writing up my instructions.

Chris Terry, an old friend, has shot the most beautiful photographs and has been a great travel companion. His assistant Danny has been amazing too.

At Penguin, John Hamilton has produced a lovely design and Juliet Annan and Anna Steadman have given advice and support. Sarah Fraser, Ellie Smith and James Blackman have worked to produce a lovely book, and Annie Lee has copy-edited it to get rid of my worst mistakes.

Thanks, lastly, to all of our suppliers; without them none of this would be possible – thank you for being there through the good times and the bad. To Brindisa: sixteen years of cooperation, trying to deliver the best-quality products we can find in Spain. To Javier De La Hormaza (Basco Fine Foods): an exceptional person and the best one when you need those products that can only be found in the Basque Country, such as Pimientos de Gernika, Basque Txuleton and Txakoli de Getaria. To Mash: always searching for the best ingredients, always walking the extra mile, always supportive. To Natoora: always helpful and resourceful, beautiful ingredients from great people. Iberflavours: for when you need best-quality ingredients such as Iberian pork meats and milk-fed lamb – call them, you will not be disappointed. Maurice at Le Marché des Chefs: a very close and helpful supplier. They always get everything I need, even the most difficult ingredients. Wright Brothers: the best oysters in the country; amazing to work with them. Channel Fisheries: my choice when I need fish on my menu, and after fourteen years I still love working with them. Don Bocarte, for the best anchovies. Angel at Cinco Jotas, who supply all our *jamón*. Imanol at El Mandanga restaurant in Santurtzi. Thanks also to Crane Cookware for the loan of the beautiful pots and pans.

FIG TREE

UK | USA | Canada | Ireland | Australia
India | New Zealand | South Africa

Fig Tree is part of the Penguin Random House group of companies
whose addresses can be found at global.penguinrandomhouse.com.

First published 2017
001

Set in Harmonia Sans Pro, Johnston ITC Std and F37 Ginger

Printed in China

A CIP catalogue record for this book is available
from the British Library

ISBN: 978-0-241-28653-1

www.greenpenguin.co.uk

MIX
Paper from
responsible sources
FSC® C018179

Penguin Random House is committed to a
sustainable future for our business, our readers
and our planet. This book is made from Forest
Stewardship Council® certified paper.